ANNE WILLAN'S
LOOK&COOK

Perfect Pasta

ANNE WILLAN'S
LOOK&COOK

Perfect Pasta

DORLING KINDERSLEY
LONDON • NEW YORK • STUTTGART

A DORLING KINDERSLEY BOOK

Created and Produced by
CARROLL & BROWN LTD
5 Lonsdale Road
London NW6 6RA

Editorial Director Jeni Wright
Editors Norma MacMillan
Stella Vayne
Art Editor Mary Staples
Designers Lyndel Donaldson
Wendy Rogers
Lucy de Rosa
Lisa Webb

First published in Great Britain in 1992
by Dorling Kindersley Limited
9 Henrietta Street, London WC2E 8PS

A CIP catalogue record for this book is available
from the British Library
ISBN 0-86318-861-3

Reproduced by Colourscan, Singapore
Printed and bound in Italy by A. Mondadori, Verona

CONTENTS

PASTA

THE LOOK & COOK APPROACH

Welcome to **Perfect Pasta** and the *Look & Cook* series. These volumes are designed to be the simplest, most informative cookbooks you'll ever own. They are the closest I can come to sharing my personal techniques for cooking my favourite recipes, without actually being with you in the kitchen looking over your shoulder.

EQUIPMENT

Equipment and ingredients often determine whether or not you can cook a particular dish, so *Look & Cook* illustrates everything you need at the beginning of each recipe. You'll see at a glance how long a recipe takes to cook, how many servings it makes, what the finished dish looks like, and how much preparation can be done ahead. When you start to cook, you'll find the preparation and cooking are organised into easy-to-follow steps. Each stage is colour-coded and everything is shown in photographs with brief text. You will never be in doubt about what it is you are doing, why you are doing it, or how it should look.

INGREDIENTS

🍽 SERVES 8-10　🥄 WORK TIME 50-60 MINUTES　🍲 COOKING TIME 4-5 MINUTES

I've also included helpful hints and ideas under 'Anne Says.' These may list an alternative ingredient or piece of equipment, or sometimes the reason for using a certain method is explained, or there is advice on mastering a particular technique. Similarly, if there is a crucial stage in a recipe when things can go wrong, I've included some warnings called 'Take Care.'

Many of the photographs are annotated to pinpoint why certain pieces of equipment work best, or how the food should look at that stage of cooking. Because presentation is so important, a picture of the finished dish and serving suggestions are at the end of each recipe.

Thanks to all this information you can't go wrong. I'll be with you every step of the way. So please, come with me into the kitchen to look, cook and create some **Perfect Pasta** dishes.

WHY PASTA?

Pasta has never been more popular. The myriad forms of basic dough are combined with other ingredients and sauces that complement their various shapes, appearing as appetisers and accompaniments as well as main courses. Many cooks like the challenge of making their own dough. But the wide range of dried and fresh pasta available in shops ensures that you can quickly prepare any one of a panoply of pasta dishes for any occasion.

RECIPE CHOICE

Say 'pasta' and everyone thinks Italian. While Italy has produced the widest range of pasta shapes and combinations, pasta is used in many other European and Asian cuisines. North America has contributed pasta salads and other contemporary ideas.

Fresh pasta made at home is usually used in two ways: cut into noodles that are boiled and served with a sauce, or shaped with a stuffing. Often, stuffed pasta is tossed simply in melted butter or oil, or a simple sauce may be added.

Dumplings are best freshly made at home though a few, such as gnocchi, are available commercially. Extruded pastas such as spaghetti, macaroni, shells and twists are made commercially and sold dried.

When I chose the recipes for this volume, I wanted to include all the familiar pasta shapes as well as the classic fillings and sauces that are such favourites. But pasta has changed with the times and you will also find lively dishes using current ingredients such as wild mushrooms and Jerusalem artichokes.

I have covered a wide range of dishes suitable for both first and main courses, and included many vegetable-based choices in tune with today's lighter diet.

LONG, THIN NOODLES

The ever-popular fettuccine is a good choice for a variety of sauces. *Fresh Fettuccine with Tomato and Basil:* home-made egg pasta, rolled and cut by machine, with a sauce of fresh tomatoes and basil. *Fresh Fettuccine with Butter and Black Pepper:* home-made pasta, rolled and cut by hand, at its simple best with butter and freshly ground black pepper. *Fettuccine with Pancetta and Egg:* the classic fettuccine *alla carbonara*. *Fettuccine Alfredo:* a pasta indulgence – rich with cream and cheese. *Fettuccine with Olives and Capers:* fresh pasta tossed with a piquant sauce. *Black Pepper Fettuccine with Three-Cheese Sauce:* black pepper adds kick to fresh pasta dough, balanced by a silky sauce of Gorgonzola, ricotta and Parmesan. *Black Pepper Fettuccine with Cheese and Chive Sauce:* chives and cheese offset the pepper's bite.

The thinner but wider tagliatelle, the best-known flat shape, is a specialty of Bologna. *Tomato Tagliatelle with Artichokes and Walnuts:* pasta dough coloured with tomato purée topped with chopped walnuts and globe artichokes. *Tomato Tagliatelle with Jerusalem Artichokes and Walnuts:* Jerusalem artichokes add the same rich flavour as globe artichokes to red tagliatelle.

I offer two choices of thinner pasta with a seafood sauce. *Spinach Linguine with White Clam Sauce*: steamed little clams served with green linguine, and *Spinach Linguine with Red Clam Sauce*: tomatoes add flavour and rich colour to this sauce.

The most delicate noodles of all are angel hair or *capellini. Angel Hair with Prawns, Asparagus and Sesame:* a light stir-fry of prawns, asparagus, ginger, spring onions and sesame seeds. *Angel Hair with Smoked Oysters, Asparagus and Sesame*: an unusual, tasty combination, uses off-the-shelf seafood to achieve a similar result.

Lastly, I've included spaghetti with its most classic accompaniments, two vegetable-based versions on the *primavera* theme and two with meat sauce. *Spaghetti with Spring Vegetables:* young, tender vegetables in a light cream sauce. *Spaghetti Verde:* spaghetti with vegetables in a variety of green tones. *Spaghetti Bolognese:* typical northern Italian fare – an ideal feast for friends. *Spaghetti with Spicy Meat Sauce:* laced with fiery hot chilli sauce.

SHORT, SHAPED PASTA

A wide range of shaped pasta is commercially available. *Corsican Macaroni with Beef Stew:* Mediterranean flavours of rosemary, garlic and cinnamon. *Macaroni with Lamb Stew:* macaroni topped with lamb and pungent green olives. *Sicilian Macaroni with Sardines, Fennel and Raisins:* flavours from sunny Sicily. *Baked Macaroni with Cheese, Fennel and Raisins:* a light filling of fennel, ricotta cheese and raisins.

Pasta quills, known as *penne* in Italian, are tubular pasta that go well with vegetables. *Quills with Autumn Vegetables:* Yellow squash, onions, tomatoes and aubergine for colour. *Three-Pepper Quills:* a trio of red, green, and yellow peppers.

Pasta twirls, or *fusilli,* are spiral-shaped noodles that catch plenty of sauce. *Curly Pasta Pesto Salad:* pesto sauce makes an excellent pasta salad. *Curly Pasta Salad with Coriander:* substitute coriander as the base for this pesto-style sauce. *Curly Pasta with Wild Mushrooms:* the earthy flavour of wild mushrooms, garlic, white wine, and cream is delicious. *Curly Pasta with Herbed Mushrooms:* sage, rosemary and thyme add fragrance.

Shells, or *conchiglie,* are natural partners for shellfish. *Shells with Shellfish Sauce:* the perfect combination spiked with garlic and chilli peppers. *Shells with Prawn Sauce:* pretty pink prawns and chopped spring onions partner pasta shells.

Farfalle (butterflies) better known as pasta bows, are the choice for my *Fresh Tuna Pasta Salad Niçoise:* cubes of grilled fresh tuna and the classic niçoise garnish of olives, green beans and tomatoes. *Vegetable Pasta Salad Niçoise:* perfect for an outdoor summer barbecue.

LAYERED AND STUFFED PASTA

Several different shapes are ideal for filling and baking. *Aubergine Lasagne with Cheese Sauce:* fresh spinach pasta is layered with baked aubergine, tomatoes, and mozzarella, echoing the colours of the Italian flag. *Aubergine Lasagne with Tomato Sauce:* another non-meat lasagne dish. *Aubergine Lasagne with Spicy Italian Sausages:* a hearty meal for a hungry crowd.

Cannelloni means 'big pipes' in Italian. *Cannelloni with Veal and Spinach:* rectangles of fresh pasta wrapped around a savoury filling of veal, spinach, bacon and cheese. *Cannelloni with Chicken and Mozzarella:* cooked chicken, mozzarella and bacon fill these rolls of fresh pasta.

Pasta takes on a new look when it is cut into slices to form contrasting spirals. *Spinach and Cheese Pinwheels on Pepper Sauce:* pasta wrapped around spinach creates an attractive pinwheel effect when sliced to serve on a striking red pepper sauce. *Spinach and Cheese Pinwheels on Parsley Sauce:* a tempting contrast of green and white, with a bright green sauce of puréed parsley.

My versions of *ravioli,* those small stuffed pasta pillows, are contemporary. *Hazelnut Ravioli with Gorgonzola Sauce:* fresh pasta filled with hazelnuts and cheese to serve in a piquant Gorgonzola cheese sauce. *Hazelnut Ravioli Soffrito:* An Italian-style garnish of aromatic vegetables for these nutty ravioli. *Crab Ravioli with Saffron Butter Sauce:* these contemporary, giant ravioli are brimming with crabmeat and served in a golden saffron sauce. *Lobster Ravioli with Saffron Butter Sauce:* another modern classic.

Tortellini are traditionally made with a cheese filling. *Cheese Tortellini with Smoked Salmon and Dill:* these little twisted stuffed pastas aren't so tricky once you try. *Cheese Tortellini with Peas:* green peas are a popular Tuscan garnish. *Cheese Tortellini with Red Pepper Sauce:* cheese-filled pastas radiate colour from the sweet red pepper sauce. *Maria's Tortellini:* this stuffing of pork, chicken, mortadella and Parma ham is one among many possibilities. *Tortellini with Caramelised Onions:* onions sautéed to a rich brown complement these meat-filled pastas.

DUMPLINGS

Pasta dough reveals its international character. *Chinese Half Moons with Lemon Sauce:* lemon is surprisingly delicious with pasta, here topping semi-circles filled with flavoured prawns and cabbage.

Italian-style dumplings or *gnocchi* are made with semolina (or flour) and baked. *Semolina Gnocchi with Cheese:* the traditional Roman accompaniment to braised beef, these dumplings, baked with butter and cheese, also make a good appetiser. *Semolina Gnocchi with Parma Ham and Pine Nuts:* toasted pine nuts and Italian ham add zest to these gnocchi.

Spaetzli, the German alternative to noodles, are batter dumplings. *Alsatian Curly Noodles with Sautéed Chicken Livers:* little dumplings from Alsace, delicious with sautéed chicken livers. *Butter-Fried Curly Noodles:* golden crisp outside and chewy inside, plain spaetzli are a good accompaniment to meat or poultry.

Totelots from Alsace are traditionally served as an appetiser or in soup. *Hot Parsley Pasta Salad:* parsley leaves silhouetted in squares of thinly-rolled fresh pasta, tossed in a spirited dressing of soured cream, vinegar, shallots and garlic. *Parsley Squares in Broth:* floating in a golden broth, these parsley squares are an elegant first course.

EQUIPMENT

When making pasta it is easy enough to mix the dough, then knead it and roll it by hand with a rolling pin, but a pasta machine will speed the job. A machine with several rollers for cutting will allow you to make various widths of noodles. A food processor can save time and effort when mixing the dough, though it must still be kneaded in a pasta machine or by hand. A plain or fluted pasta wheel is good for cutting lasagne and pasta squares for ravioli, while a pastry cutter is handy for round shapes such as tortellini.

A large stockpot or saucepan is essential because plenty of boiling water must be used for cooking pasta. For draining it, a colander is needed or you may prefer a pasta drainer that fits inside the pot. A slotted spoon can be used for removing stuffed pasta and large pieces such as lasagne so they do not split. You will also need a long-handled utensil for stirring, and a grater for grating Parmesan.

CHEESE AND PASTA

Four cheeses are commonly combined with pasta and each plays a distinctive role. Not surprisingly, they are all Italian. Parmesan is a hard cheese made from cow's milk; the best is aged at least two years so it develops an inimitable nutty piquancy. Almost always used grated, Parmesan is expensive but a little goes a long way in flavouring sauces, stuffings and sprinkled on top of cooked pasta. Freshly grated Parmesan cheese (grana is the best) is far superior to pre-grated commercial varieties.

Fresh ricotta is invaluable in stuffings because it holds other ingredients together and adds body to a mixture. It has a light, slightly granular texture and a mild taste. An acceptable substitute can be made by puréeing cottage cheese with a little cream.

True buffalo mozzarella is rare even in Italy and most now is made from cow's milk. It is the king of cheeses for melting on top of baked pastas. However, its flavour is mild and Italian fontina, bel paese or any of the mild, soft French cheeses can be used as replacements.

Blue-veined Gorgonzola is often crumbled into fillings or melted in sauces to add richness and a salty bite. Similar types include Roquefort, Danish blue (tarter and less rich), and the creamy but mild Bresse bleu. Hard blue cheeses such as Stilton are less satisfactory substitutes for Gorgonzola.

INGREDIENTS

Pasta is expressly designed to mix with other ingredients. At its simplest, it can be tossed with melted butter or olive oil, together with freshly ground pepper and perhaps some chopped herbs. Piquant ingredients like ham, pancetta, smoked fish, anchovies and olives are often added, while colourful vegetables, such as carrots, peas, green beans and courgettes appear in many contemporary recipes.

Tomato is indispensable for flavour and colour in many pasta dishes. When outdoor vine-ripened tomatoes are out of season canned plum tomatoes are an acceptable substitute.

Pasta dishes become more substantial with the addition of fish, poultry and meat; typically Italian ingredients such as spicy sausage, tuna and sardines are popular choices. And for a festive occasion, pasta with seafood such as clams, prawns, or lobster is hard to beat.

Pasta is a good provider of protein, fibre and energy-giving complex carbohydrates. You may find, however, that your diet demands some adjustments to ingredients often paired with it. Some cheeses come in low-fat forms such as reduced fat ricotta and mozzarella cheese and low-fat cottage cheese, which can be used in place of ricotta. Canned tomatoes, tomato sauce and tomato purée are available in low-salt versions. Olive oil is not only the ideal partner for pasta, but it is a healthy alternative to butter, being mono-unsaturated. Polyunsaturated margarine can also be used in place of butter, though less successfully.

TECHNIQUES

Making fresh pasta at home takes time, but the results amply justify the effort. The techniques are quite simple and in this volume I take you through them step by step, from making the dough through kneading and rolling out, to cutting a huge variety of shapes.

First is a simple egg dough, mixed either by hand or in a food processor. Then there are doughs with tomato purée, spinach and black pepper for added flavour and colour. Kneading and rolling out dough is made easy with a pasta machine, but I also show how to master these techniques by hand. Once it has been rolled out, the dough can be sliced into a variety of noodles and flat shapes, not to mention cut for special stuffed pastas such as tortellini, ravioli and cannelloni. Because pasta and sauce go hand and hand, I offer a wide variety of sauces and toppings, from basic tomato sauce to some unusual combinations.

As with the other volumes in this series, there are basic techniques for ingredients that are commonly used with pasta. You will find how to chop herbs; how to peel, seed and chop tomatoes; how to peel and chop garlic; how to chop or slice onion; how to clean and slice mushrooms; how to core, seed a pepper and cut it into strips; how to seed and dice a fresh chilli as well as instructions on making tomato sauce, and pasta dough in a food processor.

FRESH FETTUCCINE WITH TOMATO AND BASIL

Fettuccine della Casa

🍽 SERVES 6 AS AN APPETISER   🥣 WORK TIME 35-40 MINUTES*   ☕ COOKING TIME 1-2 MINUTES

EQUIPMENT

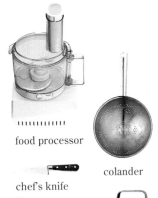

food processor

colander

chef's knife

wooden spoon

large forks

cheese grater

pasta machine

large pan

bowl

palette knife

chopping board

Here are the basics of kneading, rolling out and cutting pasta dough with a machine. This is the pasta sauce to make when juicy, sweet tomatoes are at the height of their season, with wonderful fresh basil to partner them.

GETTING AHEAD

The pasta can be made, dried and stored, loosely wrapped, in the refrigerator up to 48 hours, or it can be frozen. Sprinkle it lightly with flour or fine cornmeal so that the pieces do not stick together. Make the fresh tomato sauce and cook the fettuccine just before serving.

* plus 2-3 hours standing and drying time

INGREDIENTS

tomatoes

garlic clove

eggs

fresh basil

Parmesan cheese

flour

extra-virgin olive oil

vegetable oil

ANNE SAYS

'This sauce demands a good-quality extra-virgin olive oil because with such a simple preparation the ingredients must be the best.'

ORDER OF WORK

1 MAKE, KNEAD AND ROLL OUT, AND CUT THE DOUGH

2 MAKE THE FRESH TOMATO SAUCE

3 COOK THE FETTUCCINE AND FINISH THE DISH

metric	SHOPPING LIST	imperial
	For the pasta dough	
300 g	strong plain flour, more if needed	10 oz
3	eggs	3
15 ml	vegetable oil	1 tbsp
5 ml	salt	1 tsp
	For the fresh tomato sauce	
1	large bunch of fresh basil	1
1	garlic clove	1
4-6	large, ripe tomatoes, total weight 900 g (2 lb)	4-6
125 ml	extra-virgin olive oil	4 fl oz
	salt and pepper	
125 g	grated Parmesan cheese for serving	4 oz

1 MAKE, KNEAD AND ROLL OUT, AND CUT THE DOUGH

1 Make the pasta dough with the flour, eggs, vegetable oil and salt in the food processor (see box, page 16). Alternatively, make the dough by hand (see page 15).

2 Using the palette knife, cut the ball of pasta dough into 3 or 4 pieces of more or less equal size.

ANNE SAYS
'If you lightly flour the palette knife, it will cut more cleanly through the pasta dough.'

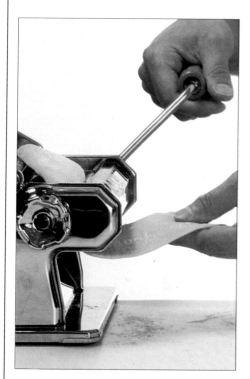

3 Set the pasta machine rollers on their widest setting. Flour one piece of dough lightly and feed it through the rollers.

4 Fold the dough strip into thirds or quarters to make a square, then feed it through the machine rollers again, dusting with flour if the dough sticks. Repeat this folding and rolling process 7-10 times to knead the dough, until it is smooth and elastic.

ANNE SAYS
'When the dough is ready, it will be satiny smooth and no longer cracking at the sides as it comes out of the rollers.'

5 Tighten the rollers one notch and feed the dough through them. Continue rolling the pasta dough, tightening the rollers one notch each time, ending with the narrowest setting. Lightly dust the dough with flour if necessary so that it does not stick to the rollers.

ANNE SAYS
'*Do not fold the pasta strip between each rolling as you did when kneading the dough.*'

Let each strip of pasta dry briefly before cutting it

6 Hang the sheet of pasta over a clean broom handle, or over the edge of the work surface, and leave to dry until the pasta has a leathery look, 5-10 minutes. Meanwhile, knead and roll out the remaining pieces of dough.

7 Cut the sheets of dough into 30 cm (12 inch) lengths with the chef's knife. Fit the handle into the wider of the machine's cutters and feed one sheet of dough through the machine. As the fettuccine strips emerge, catch them on your hand.

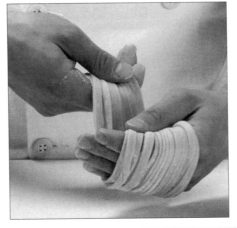

8 Toss the fettuccine with a little flour or fine cornmeal, then coil loosely into a bundle. Repeat with the remaining sheets of dough, then leave the fettuccine to dry 1-2 hours.

2 MAKE THE FRESH TOMATO SAUCE

1 Strip the basil leaves from the stalks and chop them coarsely. Finely chop the garlic.

2 Coarsely chop the tomatoes without peeling or seeding them.

3 Put the tomatoes, basil and garlic in the bowl and stir in the olive oil in a thin, steady stream. Add seasoning to taste.

3 COOK THE FETTUCCINE AND FINISH THE DISH

2 Put the fettuccine in a warmed large serving bowl, add the fresh tomato sauce and toss together with the large forks. Serve with freshly grated Parmesan cheese.

1 Fill the large pan with water, bring to the boil, and add 15 ml (1 tbsp) salt. Add the fettuccine and simmer until tender but still chewy, about 1-2 minutes, stirring occasionally to prevent sticking. Drain the fettuccine in the colander, rinse with hot water, and drain again thoroughly.

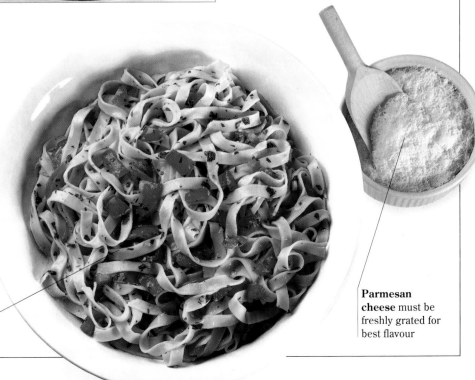

Fresh tomato sauce made with pungent basil and good-quality olive oil is perfect with pasta

Parmesan cheese must be freshly grated for best flavour

FRESH FETTUCCINE WITH BUTTER AND BLACK PEPPER

 SERVES 6 AS AN APPETISER   WORK TIME 35-40 MINUTES* COOKING TIME 1-2 MINUTES

EQUIPMENT

large pan

chef's knife

colander

palette knife**

large forks

sieve

bowl

tea towel

rolling pin

large heatproof bowl

wooden spoon

** pastry scraper can also be used

ANNE SAYS
'*Although experienced Italian cooks use a long, thin rolling pin with tapered ends, at home an ordinary rolling pin is a suitable substitute.*'

In this recipe, the pasta dough is kneaded, rolled out and cut by hand, but a pasta machine can be used instead (see pages 11-12). Hand-rolled pasta tends to be hearty, somewhat thicker than when rolled by machine. A simple topping of butter and freshly ground black pepper displays handmade pasta at its best.

GETTING AHEAD

The pasta can be made, dried and stored, loosely wrapped, in the refrigerator up to 48 hours, or it can be frozen. Sprinkle it lightly with flour or fine cornmeal so that the pieces do not stick together. Cook it just before serving.

* plus 2-3 hours standing and drying time

metric	SHOPPING LIST	imperial
	For the pasta dough	
300 g	strong plain flour, more if needed	10 oz
3	eggs	3
15 ml	vegetable oil	1 tbsp
5 ml	salt	1 tsp
	To finish	
90 g	butter	3 oz
	salt and freshly ground black pepper	

INGREDIENTS

flour

eggs

vegetable oil

butter

black peppercorns

ORDER OF WORK

1 MAKE THE PASTA DOUGH

2 KNEAD THE PASTA DOUGH

3 ROLL OUT THE PASTA DOUGH

4 CUT THE PASTA INTO STRIPS

5 COOK THE PASTA AND FINISH THE DISH

1 MAKE THE PASTA DOUGH

1 Sift the flour on to the work surface in a mound, using the sieve.

2 With your fingers, make a well in the centre of the flour.

! TAKE CARE !
Be sure the wall of flour around the well has no gaps or the eggs will run out over the work surface.

3 Add the eggs to the well in the flour, followed by the oil and salt.

Break eggs into bowl first to avoid any egg shell being added

4 Mix the eggs, oil and salt together well with your fingertips.

ANNE SAYS
'Blend the eggs with the oil before mixing in the flour.'

Palette knife provides invaluable help when mixing in flour

5 Gradually mix in the flour from the sides to make a firm dough. If the dough is sticky, add more flour.

6 Use the palette knife to scrape up bits of dough that stick to the work surface. Press the dough together into a ball.

ANNE SAYS
'Use a food processor for a quick alternative to making pasta dough by hand – see box, page 16.'

HOW TO MAKE DOUGH IN A FOOD PROCESSOR

1 Put the flour and salt into the bowl of a food processor. Add the oil and 1 egg and pulse the machine about 30 seconds.

2 Add another egg and pulse the machine a few times to mix. Add the last egg and continue working until the dough is thoroughly mixed, 1-2 minutes. (It will not form a ball.)

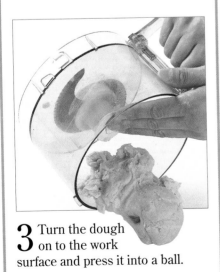

3 Turn the dough on to the work surface and press it into a ball.

2 KNEAD THE PASTA DOUGH

1 Using the palette knife, divide the dough into 2 pieces.

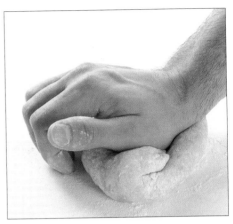

2 Put one piece on the floured work surface and knead by pushing the dough away from you with the heel of your hand.

Exert pressure with heel of hand

3 Lift the dough from the work surface, give it a half turn and push it away from you again. Continue kneading until the dough is elastic and peels from the work surface in one piece, 5-10 minutes. Knead the second piece in the same way.

4 Press all the dough together into a ball, cover with the upturned bowl, and leave to stand at room temperature 1 hour.

Cover dough to keep it moist

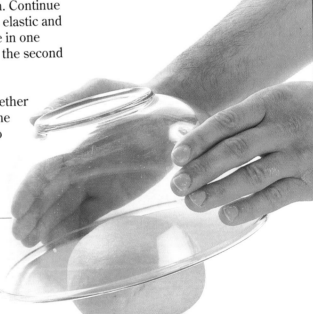

3 ROLL OUT THE PASTA DOUGH

1 Sprinkle the work surface lightly with flour. Pat the dough into a circle with the rolling pin.

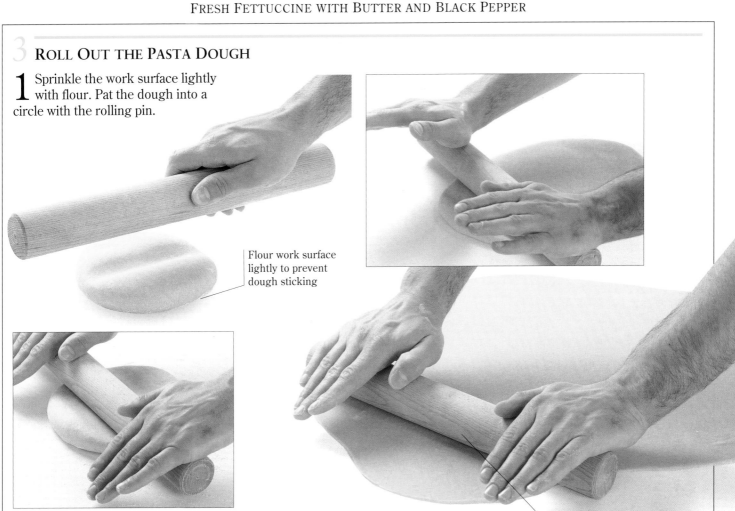

Flour work surface lightly to prevent dough sticking

Keep pressure even on rolling pin

2 Start rolling the dough, turning and moving it so that it does not stick to the surface.

ANNE SAYS
'The dough should be elastic and quite hard to roll.'

3 Continue rolling the dough to about the thickness of a postcard, keeping it in a rough circle. Sprinkle the work surface and rolling pin quite generously with flour – the dough should look velvety.

Sheet of dough on broom handle has air circulating round it so it will dry quickly

ANNE SAYS
'Instead of hanging the dough over the broom handle to dry, as here, you can hang it over the edge of your work surface and anchor it with the rolling pin.'

4 Hang the dough over a clean broom handle to dry until it has a leathery look, 5-10 minutes.

4 CUT THE PASTA INTO STRIPS

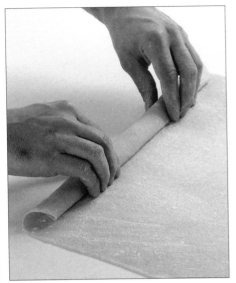

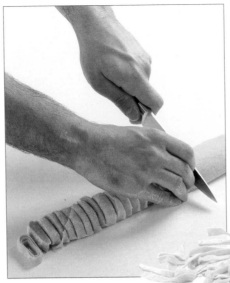

3 Unravel the fettuccine with your hands, then toss with a little flour or fine cornmeal. Leave them flat or coil loosely in bundles and leave to dry on the floured tea towel, 1-2 hours.

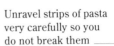

Unravel strips of pasta very carefully so you do not break them

1 For fettuccine, as shown here, sprinkle the rolled-out dough lightly with flour, then roll it up loosely into a cylinder.

2 With the chef's knife, cut the cylinder across into 5 mm (¼ inch) wide strips.

5 COOK THE PASTA AND FINISH THE DISH

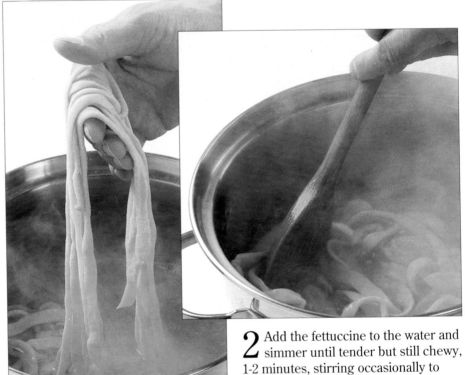

1 Fill the large pan with water. Bring the water to the boil and then add 15 ml (1 tbsp) salt.

2 Add the fettuccine to the water and simmer until tender but still chewy, 1-2 minutes, stirring occasionally to prevent sticking.

Tip pasta into colander

3 Drain the fettuccine in the colander.

4 Rinse the pasta with hot water to wash away the starch and drain again thoroughly.

🍽 **TO SERVE**
Spoon the pasta on to warmed individual plates and serve immediately.

5 Put the hot pasta in the warmed large bowl. Add the butter, cut into small pieces, and grind black pepper to taste over the top. Toss until all the strands of pasta are coated with melted butter and pepper.

Pieces of butter melt in heat of pasta

Fresh fettuccine, made by hand, simply dressed with butter and freshly ground black pepper

FETTUCCINE WITH PANCETTA AND EGG

Fettuccine alla Carbonara

 SERVES 4 OR 6 WORK TIME 35-40 MINUTES* COOKING TIME 1-2 MINUTES

EQUIPMENT

rolling pin**

palette knife

sieve

wooden spoon

cheese grater

large bowl

large pan

frying pan

chef's knife

bowls

large forks

chopping board

colander

** pasta machine can also be used

The name 'carbonara' might come from the charcoal vendors who are said to have invented this dish, or it might refer to the sprinkling of pepper, resembling carbon, on top.

GETTING AHEAD

The pasta can be made, dried and stored, loosely wrapped, in the refrigerator up to 48 hours, or it can be frozen. Sprinkle it lightly with flour or fine cornmeal so that the pieces do not stick together. The fettuccine should be cooked and the carbonara sauce made just before serving.

* plus 2-3 hours standing and drying time

metric	SHOPPING LIST	imperial
	For the pasta dough	
300 g	strong plain flour, more if needed	10 oz
3	eggs	3
15 ml	vegetable oil	1 tbsp
5 ml	salt	1 tsp
	For the carbonara sauce	
2	garlic cloves	2
a few	sprigs of parsley	a few
250 g	sliced pancetta or smoked bacon	8 oz
30 g	butter	1 oz
60 ml	dry white wine	4 tbsp
4	eggs	4
90 g	grated Parmesan cheese	3 oz
	salt and freshly ground black pepper	

INGREDIENTS

pancetta

eggs

Parmesan cheese

black peppercorns

flour

vegetable oil

butter

white wine

parsley sprigs

garlic cloves

ORDER OF WORK

1 MAKE, KNEAD AND ROLL OUT, AND CUT THE DOUGH

2 MAKE THE CARBONARA SAUCE

3 COOK THE FETTUCCINE AND FINISH THE DISH

1 MAKE, KNEAD AND ROLL OUT, AND CUT THE DOUGH

1 Make the pasta dough (see page 15). Knead, roll out and cut the dough by hand (see pages 16-18), rolling it out to about the thickness of a postcard and cutting it into 5 mm (¼ inch) wide strips. Alternatively, knead, roll out and cut the dough using a pasta machine (see pages 11-12), ending with the rollers at the narrowest setting and using the wider of the machine's cutters.

Toss the fettuccine gently with a little flour or fine cornmeal, then coil them loosely in bundles or leave them flat. Leave to dry on a floured tea towel, 1-2 hours.

ANNE SAYS
'You can use 500 g (1 lb) fresh or dried commercially-prepared fettuccine. If using dried, cook 7-10 minutes, or according to packet instructions.'

Cut dough wide or narrow as you prefer, then unwind gently

2 MAKE THE CARBONARA SAUCE

1 Chop the garlic. Chop the parsley (see box, page 22). Cut the slices of pancetta, or bacon rashers, crosswise into strips, removing the rind first, if you like.

ANNE SAYS
'To make the sauce even richer, add 30-45 ml (2-3 tbsp) double cream to the egg and cheese mixture.'

Fresh Parmesan cheese, coarsely grated, is superior in flavour to packaged versions and gives better texture

2 Melt the butter in the frying pan, add the garlic and pancetta and sauté 1-2 minutes. Add the wine and cook until reduced to 30 ml (2 tbsp). Remove from the heat and keep warm.

3 Put the eggs in the large bowl and add the grated Parmesan cheese. Season with pepper and beat well to mix with a large fork.

HOW TO CHOP HERBS

Parsley, dill, chives, rosemary, thyme and basil are herbs that are usually chopped before being added to other ingredients. Do not chop delicate herbs like basil too finely because they bruise easily.

1 Strip the leaves or sprigs from the stalks. Pile the leaves or sprigs on a chopping board.

2 With a chef's knife, cut the leaves or sprigs into pieces.

ANNE SAYS
'When chopping a large quantity of herbs, or sprigs of herbs such as the parsley shown here, hold the herbs together in a bunch with your other hand while chopping.'

3 Holding the tip of the blade against the board and rocking the blade back and forth, continue chopping until the herbs are coarse or fine, as you wish.

3 COOK THE FETTUCCINE AND FINISH THE DISH

1 Fill the large pan with water, bring to the boil and add 15 ml (1 tbsp) salt. Add the fettuccine and simmer until tender but still chewy, about 1-2 minutes, stirring occasionally to prevent sticking. Drain the pasta in the colander, rinse with hot water to wash away the starch, and drain again.

2 Add the pasta to the egg and cheese mixture and toss quickly to coat evenly.

ANNE SAYS
'The pasta must be very hot so the eggs cook and thicken slightly.'

3 Add the hot pancetta mixture to the pasta and toss to mix. Add the chopped parsley and toss again. Taste for seasoning.

ANNE SAYS
'Salt may not be needed because the pancetta and cheese are salty.'

🍴 TO SERVE
Pile the fettuccine in a warmed serving bowl or on plates and sprinkle generously with freshly ground black pepper.

VARIATION
FETTUCCINE ALFREDO

A real Italian favourite, this sauce has no bacon or eggs but uses cream for richness and flavour.

Freshly ground black pepper adds flavour to creamy rich Alfredo sauce

1 Make the pasta as for Fettuccine with Pancetta and Egg.
2 Melt 60 g (2 oz) butter in a small pan.

3 Add 250 ml (8 fl oz) double cream and bring almost to the boil.
4 Cook, drain and rinse the fettuccine as directed in the main recipe; return it to the cooking pan.
5 Pour the butter and cream mixture over the fettuccine and heat gently, tossing until the pasta is coated, about 1 minute.

6 Add 60 g (2 oz) grated Parmesan cheese to the pasta and continue tossing until the mixture is very hot, about 30 seconds. Taste for seasoning.
7 Pile the fettuccine on warmed individual plates and grind black pepper generously over the top. Serve with more grated Parmesan cheese.

VARIATION
FETTUCCINE WITH OLIVES AND CAPERS

Fettuccine Piccante

Here black olives, capers, garlic and olive oil make a piquant sauce for pasta.

1 Chop 3 garlic cloves.
2 Chop 60 g (2 oz) stoned black olives.
3 Make and cook the pasta as directed in Fettuccine with Pancetta and Egg.
4 While the pasta is cooking, in a large pan, heat 75 ml (2 ½ fl oz) fruity olive oil. Add the garlic, olives and 45 g (1½ oz) drained capers. Heat, stirring, until aromatic, about 1 minute.
5 Drain and rinse the fettuccine, add it to the garlic mixture and toss until thoroughly coated.
6 Pile the fettuccine on warmed individual plates and serve immediately.
7 If you like, garnish with extra capers and chopped black olives, in small piles on the plate.

BLACK PEPPER FETTUCCINE WITH THREE-CHEESE SAUCE

EQUIPMENT

pasta machine

large forks

small saucepan

chef's knife

palette knife

sieve

large pan

plastic bags

rolling pin without handles

wooden spoon

cheese grater

bowls

chopping board

colander

large plate

tea towel

This dish gives plain pasta dough the kick of freshly cracked black pepper, mellowed by a creamy cheese sauce. A simple green salad, tossed with a lemony dressing, would be a good accompaniment. If you want to substitute commercially-prepared pasta, season the sauce well with freshly ground black pepper.

GETTING AHEAD

The pasta can be made, dried and stored, loosely wrapped, in the refrigerator up to 48 hours, or it can be frozen. Sprinkle it lightly with flour or fine cornmeal so that the pieces do not stick together. The fettuccine should be cooked and the cheese sauce made just before serving.

* plus 2-3 hours standing and drying time

INGREDIENTS

Gorgonzola cheese

ricotta cheese

eggs

Parmesan cheese

double cream   vegetable oil

black peppercorns   flour

ANNE SAYS

'You can use 500 g (1 lb) plain fresh or dried commercially-prepared fettuccine. If using dried, cook 7-10 minutes or according to packet instructions.'

ORDER OF WORK

1 MAKE, KNEAD AND ROLL OUT, AND CUT THE BLACK PEPPER DOUGH

2 MAKE THE THREE-CHEESE SAUCE

3 COOK THE FETTUCCINE AND FINISH THE DISH

metric	SHOPPING LIST	imperial
	For the black pepper pasta dough	
30 ml	black peppercorns	2 tbsp
300 g	strong plain flour, more if needed	10 oz
3	eggs	3
15 ml	vegetable oil	1 tbsp
5 ml	salt	1 tsp
	For the three-cheese sauce	
125 g	Gorgonzola cheese	4 oz
175 ml	double cream	6 fl oz
60 g	grated Parmesan cheese	2 oz
125 g	ricotta cheese	4 oz

1 MAKE, KNEAD AND ROLL OUT, AND CUT THE BLACK PEPPER DOUGH

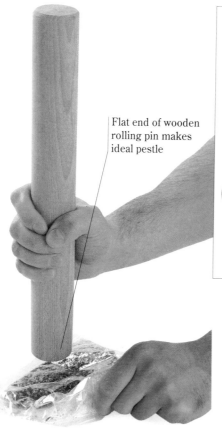

Flat end of wooden rolling pin makes ideal pestle

Ground pepper should not be too fine in texture

1 Put the peppercorns in a double thickness of plastic bags and crush with the rolling pin. Alternatively, grind the peppercorns on the coarse setting of a pepper mill or in an electric coffee grinder or spice mill.

ANNE SAYS
'You can substitute ground for fresh pepper in this recipe but it will lack aromatic pungency.'

2 Make the pasta dough (see page 15), adding the crushed pepper with the eggs, oil and salt.

Coil noodles loosely into bundles so they take up less room on work surface

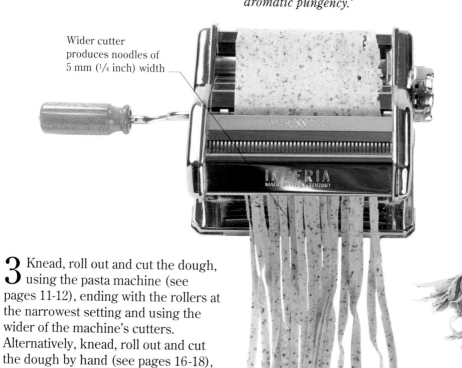

Wider cutter produces noodles of 5 mm (¼ inch) width

3 Knead, roll out and cut the dough, using the pasta machine (see pages 11-12), ending with the rollers at the narrowest setting and using the wider of the machine's cutters. Alternatively, knead, roll out and cut the dough by hand (see pages 16-18), rolling it out to the thickness of a postcard and cutting it into 5 mm (¼ inch) wide strips.

4 Toss the fettuccine gently with a little flour or fine cornmeal, then coil loosely in bundles or leave flat. Leave the pasta to dry on the floured tea towel, 1-2 hours.

2 MAKE THE THREE-CHEESE SAUCE

Three Italian cheeses are melted together with cream

ANNE SAYS
'*Stir the sauce occasionally until it is quite smooth; a few lumps of unmelted cheese will add interest.*'

1 With the chef's knife, cut the Gorgonzola cheese into small pieces, discarding any rind.

2 Put the cream in the saucepan and add the Gorgonzola, Parmesan and ricotta. Heat gently, stirring, until all 3 cheeses are melted, 2-3 minutes. Do not overheat.

3 COOK THE FETTUCCINE AND FINISH THE DISH

Adding coils of pasta to pan one at a time is easier than adding handfuls of dangling noodles

Black pepper fettuccine is coiled in bundles so it can be dropped easily into boiling water

1 Fill the large pan with water, bring to the boil and add 15 ml (1 tbsp) salt. Add the fettuccine and simmer until tender but still chewy, about 1-2 minutes, stirring occasionally to prevent sticking. Drain the pasta in the colander, rinse with hot water to wash away the starch, and drain again.

2 Transfer the hot pasta to a warmed large bowl. Pour the cheese sauce over the pasta.

Serving bowl should be warmed beforehand to prevent pasta and sauce cooling too quickly

3 Toss the fettuccine and cheese sauce together with the large forks until all the strands of pasta are coated with the sauce. Taste for seasoning and serve immediately.

Gorgonzola and ricotta cheeses dot pasta, while Parmesan melts into sauce

VARIATION
BLACK PEPPER FETTUCCINE WITH CHEESE AND CHIVE SAUCE

The onion taste of chives is substituted for the Gorgonzola, adding pungency of a different dimension.

1 Omit the Gorgonzola cheese.
2 Chop a small bunch of chives and stir them into the sauce just before tossing with the fettuccine.

Bright green chives add colour and pungent flavour to creamy sauce

Flecks of black pepper can be seen clearly in fettuccine

SPINACH LINGUINE WITH WHITE CLAM SAUCE

🍽 SERVES 4 OR 6　🥄 WORK TIME 50-60 MINUTES*　🍲 COOKING TIME 1-2 MINUTES

EQUIPMENT

food processor

colander

sieve

flameproof casserole

palette knife

stiff brush

chef's knife

heatproof bowl

wooden spoon

slotted spoon

bowls

frying pan

small saucepan

tea towel

large pan

pasta machine

White clam sauce provides a natural contrast to green spinach pasta. If small, succulent clams are out of season, mussels can be used instead.

GETTING AHEAD

The pasta can be made, dried and stored, loosely wrapped, in the refrigerator up to 48 hours, or it can be frozen. Sprinkle it lightly with flour or fine cornmeal so that the pieces do not stick together. The clam sauce can be prepared up to 6 hours ahead and refrigerated. Reheat it and cook the linguine at the last minute.

* plus 2-3 hours standing and drying time

metric	SHOPPING LIST	imperial
	For the spinach pasta dough	
90 g	fresh spinach	3 oz
300 g	strong plain flour, more if needed	10 oz
3	eggs	3
15 ml	vegetable oil	1 tbsp
5 ml	salt	1 tsp
	For the clam sauce	
3.6 kg	clams	8 lb
1	onion	1
250 ml	dry white wine	8 fl oz
2	garlic cloves	2
a few	sprigs of parsley	a few
60 ml	olive oil	4 tbsp
	salt and pepper	

INGREDIENTS

fresh spinach　　eggs

garlic cloves

onion

olive oil

flour

parsley sprigs　　clams

vegetable oil　white wine

ANNE SAYS
'You can replace fresh clams with two 250 g (8 oz) cans clams. Use liquid from cans instead of cooking liquid.'

ORDER OF WORK

1　MAKE, KNEAD AND ROLL OUT, AND CUT THE SPINACH DOUGH

2　MAKE THE CLAM SAUCE

3　COOK THE LINGUINE AND FINISH THE DISH

1 MAKE, KNEAD AND ROLL OUT, AND CUT THE SPINACH DOUGH

Flour tea towel so pasta does not stick

1 Discard the tough ribs and stalks from the spinach, then wash it thoroughly. Fill the small pan with salted water and bring to the boil. Add the spinach and simmer until tender, 2-3 minutes. Drain the spinach in the colander, rinse with cold water and drain again thoroughly. Squeeze the spinach in your hand to remove all excess water. Purée the spinach in the food processor, or chop it very finely with the chef's knife. You should have about 45 ml (3 tbsp).

! TAKE CARE !
The spinach must be thoroughly drained or the resulting dough will be sticky and hard to work.

2 Make the pasta dough (see page 15), adding the spinach with the eggs, oil and salt. Knead, roll out and cut the dough using the pasta machine (see pages 11-12), ending with the rollers at the narrowest setting and using the narrower of the machine's cutters. Alternatively, knead, roll out and cut the dough by hand (see pages 16-18), rolling it out to about the thickness of a postcard and cutting it into 3 mm (¹/₈ inch) wide strips.

ANNE SAYS
'*If you make the pasta dough using a food processor, it will have an even green colour. Made by hand using finely chopped spinach, the dough will be speckled green.*'

3 Toss the linguine gently with a little flour or fine cornmeal, then coil it loosely in bundles, or leave it flat, and spread out on the floured tea towel. Leave it to dry, 1-2 hours.

ANNE SAYS
'*You may prefer to save time and buy commercially-prepared pasta; allow 500 g (1 lb) fresh or dried linguine. If using dried pasta, cook 7-10 minutes, or according to packet instructions.*'

2 MAKE THE CLAM SAUCE

1 Scrub the clams under cold running water. Discard any clams that have broken shells or that do not close when tapped.

ANNE SAYS
'*If the clams are very sandy, clean them by putting them in a large bowl of water with salt and flour, allowing 15 ml (1 tbsp) of each per litre (1³/₄ pints) water. Leave 1-2 hours, then drain and rinse the clams under cold running water.*'

Use stiff-bristled brush to scrub clam shells clean

2 Put the clams in the casserole or in a large saucepan. Finely chop the onion and add to the casserole with the wine. Cover and cook over high heat, shaking the casserole occasionally, until the shells open, 5-8 minutes. (Cooking time depends on the thickness of the shells.) Discard any clams that have not opened.

3 Lift out the clams with the slotted spoon and put them in a bowl. Set them aside to cool slightly.

4 Reduce the cooking liquid over high heat to about 250 ml (8 fl oz), then pour it into a small bowl, leaving any sand at the bottom of the pan.

Use your fingers to take clams from opened shells

5 Remove the clams from their shells, reserving 2 or 3 in their shells to garnish each serving.

! TAKE CARE !
Discard any clams that have not opened.

6 Finely chop the garlic. Chop the parsley, reserving a few good sprigs for garnish.

7 Heat the oil in the frying pan, add the garlic and sauté 30 seconds; do not let it brown. Add the steamed clams, chopped parsley and the reduced cooking liquid and stir with the wooden spoon to mix. Season to taste with salt and pepper.

Clam cooking liquid is reduced to concentrate flavour before being added to sauce mixture

Tender clams need no more cooking, just reheating

8 Add the reserved clams in shells. Cover the pan and remove from the heat.

Add clams in shells to sauce for reheating

3 COOK THE LINGUINE AND FINISH THE DISH

1 Fill the large pan with water, bring to the boil and add 15 ml (1 tbsp) salt. Add the linguine and simmer until tender but still chewy, 1-2 minutes, stirring occasionally to prevent sticking. Meanwhile, reheat the clam sauce. Drain the linguine in the colander, rinse with hot water to wash away the starch, and drain again thoroughly.

🍽 TO SERVE
Transfer the linguine to the warmed heatproof bowl, pour the warm clam sauce over the linguine and toss to mix. Pile on individual plates. Add the clams in their shells plus a few sprigs of parsley for garnish.

VARIATION

SPINACH LINGUINE WITH RED CLAM SAUCE

Tomatoes add lovely colour to this variation of Spinach Linguine with White Clam Sauce.

1 Peel, seed and chop 1 kg (2 lb) tomatoes.
2 Add the tomatoes to the sautéed garlic in step 7 of making the sauce. Simmer, stirring occasionally, until thickened, 15-20 minutes, then add the clams, parsley and cooking liquid.
3 Cook, drain and rinse the linguine as directed; arrange in a warmed large serving bowl and spoon the sauce in the centre. Garnish with the clams in their shells.

ANNE SAYS
'If you have made the clam sauce ahead of time, when reheating it, be sure not to overcook the clams or they will be tough.'

TOMATO TAGLIATELLE WITH ARTICHOKES AND WALNUTS

🍽 SERVES 4 OR 6   🥣 WORK TIME 50-60 MINUTES*   ♨ COOKING TIME 3-4 MINUTES

EQUIPMENT

pasta machine**

sieve

palette knife

wooden spoon

medium saucepan

large forks

bowls

large frying pan

cheese grater

chef's knife

small knife

teaspoon

large pan

heatproof plate

chopping board

colander

** rolling pin can also be used

The nutty flavour of artichokes, sliced and sautéed in garlic and olive oil, is good with pasta. Use an extra-virgin olive oil so the flavour of the finished dish is intense.

GETTING AHEAD

The pasta can be made, dried and stored, loosely wrapped, in the refrigerator up to 48 hours, or it can be frozen. Sprinkle it lightly with flour or fine cornmeal so that the pieces do not stick together. The tagliatelle should be cooked and the topping prepared just before serving.

* plus 2-3 hours standing and drying time

metric	SHOPPING LIST	imperial
	For the tomato pasta dough	
300 g	strong plain flour, more if needed	10 oz
37.5 ml	tomato purée	2 ½ tbsp
3	eggs	3
15 ml	vegetable oil	1 tbsp
5 ml	salt	1 tsp
	For the artichoke topping	
6	large globe artichokes	6
2	lemons	2
4	garlic cloves	4
2	shallots	2
1	small bunch of parsley	1
45 g	walnut halves	1 ½ oz
75 ml	extra-virgin olive oil	5 tbsp
45 ml	dry white wine	3 tbsp
	salt and pepper	
30 g	grated Parmesan cheese	1 oz

INGREDIENTS

eggs

globe artichokes

flour

walnuts

shallots

vegetable oil

Parmesan cheese

white wine

lemons

tomato purée

parsley

garlic cloves

olive oil

ORDER OF WORK

1. MAKE, KNEAD AND ROLL OUT, AND CUT THE DOUGH

2. MAKE THE ARTICHOKE TOPPING

3. COOK THE TAGLIATELLE AND FINISH THE DISH

1 MAKE, KNEAD AND ROLL OUT, AND CUT THE DOUGH

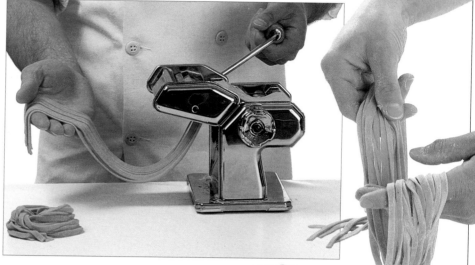

1 Make the pasta dough (see page 15), adding the tomato purée with the eggs, oil and salt.

ANNE SAYS
'You may prefer to save time and buy commercially-prepared pasta; allow 500 g (1 lb) fresh or dried tagliatelle. If you cannot find tomato tagliatelle, plain egg tagliatelle is perfectly acceptable. If using dried pasta, cook 7-10 minutes or according to packet instructions.'

2 Knead, roll out and cut the dough using the pasta machine (see pages 11-12), ending with the rollers at the second narrowest setting and using the wider of the machine's cutters. Alternatively, knead, roll out and cut the dough by hand (see pages 16-18), rolling it out to about the thickness of a table knife blade and cutting the dough into 5 mm (¼ inch) wide strips.

3 Toss the tagliatelle gently with a little flour or fine cornmeal, then coil loosely in bundles. Leave to dry on a floured tea towel 1-2 hours.

2 MAKE THE ARTICHOKE TOPPING

1 Prepare and cook the artichoke bottoms (see box, page 34). Cut them in half and slice each half thickly.

ANNE SAYS
'As a short cut, you can replace the fresh artichokes with 6 frozen or canned artichoke bottoms. Cook frozen bottoms according to packet instructions, or drain canned ones.'

2 With the chef's knife, finely chop the garlic and finely chop the shallots.

3 Chop the parsley. Roughly chop the walnuts.

Warm artichokes gently so they absorb flavourings but do not break up

4 Heat the olive oil in the frying pan. Add the shallots and garlic and sauté gently until soft but not brown, about 1 minute.

5 Add the artichokes and white wine and simmer 2-3 minutes. Season to taste with salt and pepper.

How To Prepare and Cook Artichoke Bottoms

1 Snap the stalk from a large artichoke so that the fibres are pulled out with the stalk. Snap off the largest bottom leaves with your hands. Using a sharp knife, cut off all remaining large bottom leaves, leaving a cone of small soft leaves.

2 Cut off the soft cone of leaves, leaving only the choke behind.

3 Trim the base of any remaining green parts, then trim to an even shape, slightly flattened at the base with the edge bevelled.

Plate will keep artichokes totally immersed in water, so that they will not discolour

4 Rub the base well with a cut lemon to prevent discoloration. Immerse the artichoke in a bowl of water acidulated with the juice of half a lemon while preparing any more artichokes in the same way.

5 Put the artichoke bottoms in a pan of salted water and weigh them down with a heatproof plate. Bring the water to the boil and simmer until tender, 15-20 minutes.

6 Drain the artichoke bottoms and allow them to cool until tepid, then scoop out the chokes with a teaspoon.

3 COOK THE TAGLIATELLE AND FINISH THE DISH

Use long-handled wooden forks to lift noodles while tossing

1 Fill the large pan with water, bring to the boil and add 15 ml (1 tbsp) salt. Add the tagliatelle and simmer until tender but still chewy, about 2-3 minutes, stirring occasionally to prevent sticking. Drain the pasta in the colander, rinse with hot water to wash away the starch, and drain again thoroughly.

2 Add the drained tagliatelle to the pan containing the artichoke mixture and toss over moderate heat until the pasta is hot and evenly coated with olive oil.

🍽️ **TO SERVE** Pile the pasta on a warmed serving dish and sprinkle with the chopped parsley and walnuts, and the Parmesan cheese.

Good Parmesan is pale yellow, slightly moist, and a little salty

V A R I A T I O N

TOMATO TAGLIATELLE WITH JERUSALEM ARTICHOKES AND WALNUTS

Jerusalem artichokes have a similar flavour to globe artichokes, although they belong to different species. (A globe artichoke is a type of thistle, while Jerusalem artichokes belong to the sunflower family.)

1 Make the tomato tagliatelle as directed.
2 Replace the globe artichokes with 500 g (1 lb) Jerusalem artichokes; omit the lemons.

3 Peel the artichokes and simmer until tender, 15-20 minutes. Drain, slice and simmer in wine, as directed for globe artichokes.
4 Finish the dish as directed.

AUBERGINE LASAGNE WITH CHEESE SAUCE

 SERVES 8 AS A MAIN COURSE   WORK TIME 40-45 MINUTES*   COOKING TIME 55-75 MINUTES

EQUIPMENT

- chef's knife
- small knife
- palette knife
- food processor
- slotted spoon
- whisk
- wooden spoon
- pastry brush
- saucepans
- sieve
- colander
- 23 x 32.5 cm (9 x 13 inch) baking dish

- pasta machine**
- cheese grater
- small ladle
- bowls
- large wide pan
- baking sheets

** rolling pin can also be used

Lasagne must be the favourite Italian baked pasta. This recipe follows the traditional Northern Italian method, using a mandatory four layers of pasta and filling. Three or five layers, and some Italians won't call it lasagne!

* plus 2-3 hours standing and drying time

INGREDIENTS

- fresh spinach
- aubergines
- Parmesan cheese
- vegetable oil
- tomatoes
- eggs
- butter
- milk
- nutmeg
- mozzarella cheese
- flour

metric	SHOPPING LIST	imperial
	For the spinach pasta dough	
90 g	fresh spinach	3 oz
300 g	strong plain flour, more if needed	10 oz
3	eggs	3
15 ml	vegetable oil	1 tbsp
5 ml	salt	1 tsp
	butter for baking dish	
	For the filling	
500 g	aubergines	1 lb
	vegetable oil for baking sheets and brushing	
500 g	tomatoes	1 lb
250 g	mozzarella cheese	8 oz
	For the cheese sauce	
1 litre	milk	1⅔ pints
90 g	butter	3 oz
45 g	flour	1½ oz
	ground nutmeg	
	salt and pepper	
125 g	grated Parmesan cheese	4 oz

ORDER OF WORK

1. **MAKE THE SPINACH PASTA RECTANGLES**

2. **COOK THE SPINACH PASTA RECTANGLES**

3. **PREPARE THE FILLING**

4. **MAKE THE CHEESE SAUCE**

5. **ASSEMBLE AND BAKE THE LASAGNE**

1 MAKE THE SPINACH PASTA RECTANGLES

1 Discard the tough ribs and stalks from the spinach, then wash it thoroughly. Bring a medium pan of salted water to the boil, add the spinach and simmer until tender, 2-3 minutes. Drain the spinach in the colander, rinse with cold water and drain again thoroughly. Squeeze the spinach in your hands to remove all excess water.

! TAKE CARE !
The spinach must be thoroughly drained or the resulting dough will be sticky and hard to work.

2 Purée the spinach in the food processor, or chop it very finely with the chef's knife. You should have about 45 ml (3 tbsp).

ANNE SAYS
'You can replace the fresh spinach in the pasta dough with frozen. Cook it according to packet instructions. You will need about 45 ml (3 tbsp) drained cooked spinach.'

3 Make the pasta dough (see page 15), adding the spinach with the eggs, oil and salt.

ANNE SAYS
'If you make the pasta dough using the food processor, it will have an even green colour. If made by hand, using finely chopped spinach, the dough will be speckled green.'

4 Knead and roll out the dough using the pasta machine (see pages 11-12), ending with the rollers at the second narrowest setting. Alternatively, knead and roll out the dough by hand (see pages 16-17), rolling it out in strips about 13 cm (5 inches) wide and the thickness of a table knife blade. Allow the dough to dry until it has a leathery look, 5-10 minutes.

5 Using a ruler as a guide, cut the dough into 12 rectangles, each about 10 x 20 cm (4 x 8 inches), discarding the end pieces and rough edges. Spread out the rectangles on a floured tea towel, sprinkle them with a little flour or fine cornmeal and leave to dry, 1-2 hours.

ANNE SAYS
'If your baking dish is not exactly 23 x 32.5 cm (9 x 13 inches), cut the pasta rectangles to fit its dimensions.'

2 COOK THE SPINACH PASTA RECTANGLES

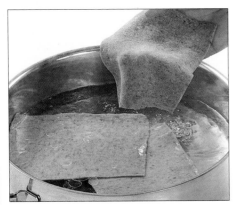

Lay lasagne rectangles flat on tea towel, not touching each other, so they can drain and dry evenly

1 Fill the large wide pan with water, bring to the boil and add 15 ml (1 tbsp) salt. Add the pasta rectangles a few at a time, and simmer until barely tender, 3-5 minutes, stirring occasionally.

ANNE SAYS
'Adding a few spoonfuls of oil to the water will help prevent the pasta rectangles sticking together.'

2 Using the slotted spoon, lift out the lasagne rectangles and put into a bowl of cold water. When cold, lift out and drain thoroughly on a clean tea towel.

3 PREPARE THE FILLING

1 Trim the ends from the aubergines, then cut them into 5 mm (¼ inch) thick slices. Put the slices in the colander and sprinkle generously with salt. Leave 30 minutes to draw out bitter juices.

2 Heat the oven to 180°C (350°F, Gas 4). Rinse the aubergine slices and pat dry with kitchen paper.

3 Oil the baking sheets. Spread out the aubergine slices on the sheets and brush them with oil.

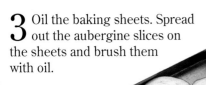

Brush aubergine slices lightly with oil, otherwise finished lasagne will be greasy

4 Bake them in the oven until tender, turning them once, 20-25 minutes.

Use your knuckles to guide knife as you slice tomatoes

5 Meanwhile, core the tomatoes and cut them into thin slices.

6 Cut the mozzarella cheese into 5 mm (¼ inch) thick slices.

4 MAKE THE CHEESE SAUCE

1 Scald the milk in a medium saucepan.

2 Melt the butter in another saucepan over moderate heat. Whisk in the flour and cook until foaming, 1-2 minutes.

Add milk when pan is off heat to prevent sauce becoming grainy

3 Remove from the heat and whisk in the hot milk. Return to the heat and cook, whisking constantly, until the sauce boils and thickens. Season with a pinch of nutmeg, salt and pepper, and simmer 2 minutes.

4 Remove the sauce from the heat and stir in three-quarters of the Parmesan cheese, reserving the rest for sprinkling.

! TAKE CARE !

Do not let the sauce boil after adding the cheese or the cheese will become stringy.

5 ASSEMBLE AND BAKE THE LASAGNE

It is all right
if edges overlap
slightly

1 Butter the baking dish. Ladle a layer of cheese sauce into the baking dish to cover the bottom.

2 Cover with a layer of lasagne rectangles and arrange half of the aubergine slices on top.

3 Ladle another layer of cheese sauce over the aubergine slices. Cover with lasagne rectangles.

Keep filling closely
packed so final servings
will have neat
appearance

4 Arrange half of the mozzarella on top, then half of the tomato slices.

5 Cover with another layer of lasagne rectangles. Continue with another layer of aubergine, then cheese sauce, then lasagne, and then another layer of mozzarella and tomato slices (you should have 4 layers of filling), ending with a generous layer of cheese sauce.

6 Sprinkle with the remaining Parmesan cheese. Bake the lasagne in the heated 180°C (350°F, Gas 4) oven until bubbling and brown, 30-45 minutes.

ANNE SAYS
'You may prefer to save time and buy commercially-prepared lasagne noodles; allow 375 g (12 oz) dried lasagne. If you cannot find spinach lasagne, plain egg lasagne is perfectly acceptable. Cook 8-10 minutes, or according to packet instructions.'

V A R I A T I O N
AUBERGINE LASAGNE WITH TOMATO SAUCE

1 Make the pasta dough, omitting the spinach. Knead, roll out, cut and cook the lasagne rectangles as directed.
2 Replace the cheese sauce with 500 ml (16 fl oz) tomato sauce.
3 Assemble the lasagne as directed, if you like using individual dishes. Add 125 g (4 oz) ricotta cheese with the aubergine slices.
4 Bake the lasagne as directed.

V A R I A T I O N
AUBERGINE LASAGNE WITH SPICY ITALIAN SAUSAGES

Spicy Italian sausages, laced with hot pepper and fennel, add a meaty twist to this classic dish.

1 Prepare the spinach lasagne rectangles, aubergines, tomatoes, mozzarella and cheese sauce as directed.
2 In a small frying pan, fry 375 g (12 oz) spicy Italian sausages, turning occasionally so that they brown and cook evenly, 10-15 minutes.
3 Drain the sausages on kitchen paper. When cool enough to handle, slice them thinly.
4 Assemble the lasagne as directed, adding the sausage slices with the layers of aubergine.
5 Sprinkle with the Parmesan cheese and bake as directed.

Parmesan cheese topping is appetisingly browned

Spinach pasta and filling make colourful layers

GETTING AHEAD
The lasagne can be prepared up to 48 hours ahead and kept refrigerated. It can also be frozen. Bake it just before serving, thawing it first if necessary.

CANNELLONI WITH VEAL AND SPINACH

 SERVES 6-8 AS A MAIN COURSE   WORK TIME 55-60 MINUTES* COOKING TIME 20-25 MINUTES

EQUIPMENT

palette knife

pasta machine

sieve

conical sieve

cheese grater

food processor

bowls

chef's knife

saucepans

rubber spatula

shallow baking dish

large wide pan

fish slice

frying pan

small ladle

Here rectangles of pasta are rolled around a filling of minced meat and spinach, then baked in a classic smooth tomato sauce.

*plus 2-3 hours standing and drying time

metric	SHOPPING LIST	imperial
	butter for dish	
30 g	grated Parmesan cheese, for topping	1 oz
	For the pasta dough	
300 g	strong plain flour, more if needed	10 oz
3	eggs	3
15 ml	vegetable oil	1 tbsp
5 ml	salt	1 tsp
	For the veal and spinach filling	
175 g	frozen leaf spinach	6 oz
300 g	boneless veal	10 oz
60 g	piece bacon or pancetta	2 oz
1	medium onion	1
15 ml	olive oil	1 tbsp
60 g	grated Parmesan cheese	2 oz
2	eggs	2
125 ml	double cream	4 fl oz
	salt and pepper	
	ground nutmeg	
	For the tomato sauce	
1 kg	tomatoes	2 lb
2	medium onions	2
3	garlic cloves	3
45 ml	vegetable oil	3 tbsp
30 ml	tomato purée	2 tbsp
1	bouquet garni	1
5 ml	sugar	1 tsp

INGREDIENTS

boneless veal

frozen leaf spinach

bacon

tomatoes

tomato purée

eggs

garlic cloves

bouquet garni

olive oil

ground nutmeg

double cream

onions

vegetable oil

Parmesan cheese

flour

sugar

ORDER OF WORK

1 PREPARE THE PASTA RECTANGLES

2 MAKE THE VEAL AND SPINACH FILLING

3 PREPARE AND BAKE THE CANNELLONI

1 PREPARE THE PASTA RECTANGLES

1 Make the pasta dough (see page 15). Knead and roll out the dough using the pasta machine (see pages 11-12), ending with the rollers at the second narrowest setting. Alternatively, knead and roll out the dough by hand (see pages 16-17), rolling it out in strips about 12.5 cm (5 inches) wide and the thickness of a knife blade.

2 Using a ruler as a guide, trim the strips of dough to a width of about 10 cm (4 inches). Cut each strip across into 7.5 cm (3 inch) long rectangles, discarding the end pieces and rough edges. There should be 24 rectangles for the final dish, but it is advisable to make extra at this stage because some rectangles may break during simmering and draining.

3 Spread out the rectangles on a floured tea towel and sprinkle them with a little flour or fine cornmeal. Allow to dry, 1-2 hours.

ANNE SAYS
'You can use commercially-prepared lasagne sheets; allow 375 g (12 oz) dried lasagne and cook 8-10 minutes, or according to packet instructions.'

2 MAKE THE VEAL AND SPINACH FILLING

Scrape down side of food processor bowl 2 or 3 times with rubber spatula

1 Cook the spinach according to packet instructions, then drain well and squeeze dry. Chop it finely.

ANNE SAYS
'You can also use chopped frozen spinach, which does not need to be cooked. Put it in the sieve and leave it to thaw, then squeeze with your hands to remove all excess water. Chard leaves, popular in Italy, are an unusual substitute for spinach. Cook like fresh spinach, then chop them finely.'

2 Cut the veal and bacon into chunks. Quarter the onion.

3 Work the veal, bacon and onion in the food processor or put through the fine blade of a mincer.

ANNE SAYS
'A mincer gives the filling a lighter texture. If you use a food processor, be sure not to purée the meat too finely.'

4 Heat the olive oil in the frying pan. Add the meat mixture and sauté over low heat, stirring constantly, until cooked and beginning to brown, 8-10 minutes. Stir in the spinach and cheese. Remove from the heat and allow to cool slightly.

5 Lightly beat the eggs and cream until blended.

6 Season the meat mixture to taste with salt, pepper and a pinch of nutmeg. Stir in the egg mixture.

ANNE SAYS
'The filling for the cannelloni can also be prepared with cooked meat in place of the veal, making this an ideal dish for using up leftovers.'

HOW TO MAKE TOMATO SAUCE

If tomatoes are out of season, looking pale and tasteless, it is better to substitute the same amount of canned tomatoes. Chop them coarsely, discarding the seeds.

1 Chop the tomatoes, but do not peel or seed them (the peel and seeds will be sieved out later). Finely chop the onions. Chop the garlic. Heat the oil in a large saucepan and sauté the onions until browned, 2-3 minutes, stirring frequently.

2 Stir in the tomatoes, garlic, tomato purée, bouquet garni, sugar, salt and pepper.

3 Cook, stirring occasionally, until fairly thick, 12-15 minutes. Strain the tomato sauce through a conical sieve into a bowl, pressing down well to extract all the tomato pulp. Taste for seasoning.

Small ladle is best utensil for pressing tomato sauce through sieve

3 PREPARE AND BAKE THE CANNELLONI

1 Make the tomato sauce (see box, page 44). Fill the large wide pan with water, bring to the boil and add 15 ml (1 tbsp) salt. Add the pasta rectangles a few at a time and simmer until barely tender, 3-5 minutes, stirring gently from time to time to prevent sticking.

ANNE SAYS
'Adding a little oil to the cooking water will help prevent the pasta rectangles sticking together.'

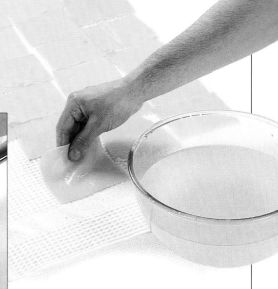

Put pasta rectangles side by side on towel

2 As the pasta rectangles are cooked, lift them out with the fish slice and put them into a bowl of cold water.

3 Lift the pasta rectangles out of the cold water and put them on a clean tea towel, not overlapping them, to drain thoroughly.

4 Butter the baking dish. Heat the oven to 200°C (400°F, Gas 6). Spoon about 30-45 ml (2-3 tbsp) of the filling on each pasta rectangle along one long edge.

5 Roll up each rectangle into a neat cylinder and pack snugly in the buttered baking dish.

ANNE SAYS
'For a dinner party, I like to bake the cannelloni in individual dishes instead of using one big baking dish.'

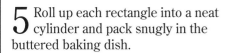

Arrange cannelloni in single layer in dish

6 Spoon the tomato sauce over the cannelloni so they are all covered.

Small ladle gives more control when spooning on sauce

Cannelloni should fit snugly in rows in baking dish

7 Sprinkle the Parmesan cheese evenly over the top. Bake the cannelloni in the heated oven until bubbling and brown, 20-25 minutes.

PARMESAN CHEESE

Parmesan is a hard cheese made from cow's milk. The best is Parmigiano-Reggiano grana, which is aged at least 2 years to develop an inimitable nutty piquancy. It is expensive, but a little goes a long way in flavouring sauces, stuffings and when sprinkled on top of cooked pasta. Freshly grated Parmesan cheese is far superior to the dry commercial varieties. Pecorino Romano is an undistinguished alternative.

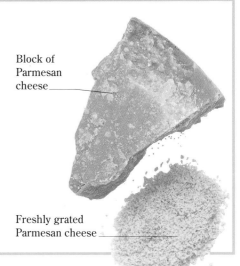

Block of Parmesan cheese

Freshly grated Parmesan cheese

🍴 TO SERVE

Cut between the cannelloni to loosen them, then lift out of the dish, using the fish slice, and arrange on warmed plates. Spoon the tomato sauce over and around and sprinkle with the Parmesan cheese.

Grated Parmesan cheese topping looks – and tastes – good with tomato sauce

— **GETTING AHEAD** —
The cannelloni can be prepared, ready for baking, up to 24 hours ahead and kept refrigerated, or they can be frozen.

CANNELLONI WITH CHICKEN AND MOZZARELLA

A delicious way to use any leftover cooked chicken you have on hand.

1 Prepare and cook the pasta rectangles as directed in Cannelloni with Veal and Spinach.
2 Omit the meat filling.
3 Cut a 125 g (4 oz) piece of mozzarella cheese into small cubes.
4 Mix 375 g (12 oz) cooked shredded chicken meat with the mozzarella cubes. Add salt and pepper to taste and 2 eggs, beaten to mix.

5 Cut 6 thin slices of bacon or pancetta into 4 strips each, discarding any pieces of bone and rind. Set one strip on each pasta rectangle.

6 Spoon about 45 ml (2-3 tbsp) chicken filling on each pasta rectangle along one long edge. Roll up the pasta and arrange in the buttered large baking dish.

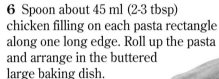

Strip of bacon will add flavour to chicken and mozzarella filling

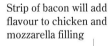

Beaten eggs will enrich chicken and mozzarella filling and bind it together

7 Add 30 ml (2 tbsp) chopped fresh basil to the tomato sauce and spoon over the cannelloni. Bake as directed. Serve sprinkled with grated Parmesan and decorated with basil.

HOT PARSLEY PASTA SALAD

Totelots au Persil

 SERVES 6 AS AN APPETISER   WORK TIME 40-45 MINUTES*   COOKING TIME 3-5 MINUTES

EQUIPMENT

large pan

sieve

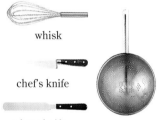

pasta machine   pastry brush

whisk

chef's knife

palette knife

colander

tea towel

bowls

chopping board

medium saucepan

rolling pin

wooden spoon

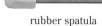

fluted pasta wheel

rubber spatula

The concept of a hot pasta salad with a cold dressing may sound new but 'totelots' is a traditional appetiser from Alsace. The new twist here is rolling leaves of flat parsley inside squares of pasta dough so they appear in silhouette. The result is very pretty indeed.

* plus 2-3 hours standing and drying time

metric	SHOPPING LIST	imperial
1	medium bunch of flat parsley	1
	For the pasta dough	
250 g	strong plain flour, more if needed	8 oz
2	eggs	2
1	egg yolk	1
30 ml	water	2 tbsp
5 ml	salt	1 tsp
	For the dressing	
2	shallots	2
1	garlic clove	1
a few	sprigs of parsley	a few
20 ml	red wine vinegar	4 tsp
37.5 ml	soured cream	2 ½ tbsp
	salt and pepper	
60 ml	vegetable oil	4 tbsp
2	eggs, for decoration	2

INGREDIENTS

garlic clove

flat parsley

shallots

flour

eggs

parsley sprigs

soured cream

red wine vinegar   vegetable oil

ANNE SAYS
'You can use chervil instead of the flat parsley.'

ORDER OF WORK

1 MAKE THE PARSLEY PASTA SQUARES

2 MAKE THE DRESSING AND PREPARE THE DECORATION

3 COOK THE PARSLEY SQUARES AND FINISH THE DISH

1 MAKE THE PARSLEY PASTA SQUARES

1 Make the pasta dough (see page 15), adding the egg yolk and water in place of 1 egg and omitting the oil. Knead and roll out the dough using the pasta machine (see pages 11-12), ending with the rollers at the narrowest setting. Alternatively, knead and roll out the dough by hand (see pages 16-17), rolling it out in strips about 13 cm (5 inches) wide and about the thickness of a postcard.

2 With your fingers, carefully pull the leaves from the stalks of flat parsley.

3 Brush halfway along one of the strips of pasta dough very lightly with water.

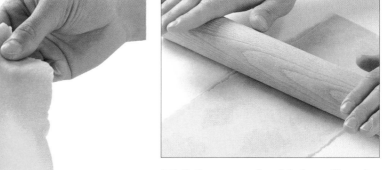

4 Arrange the flat parsley leaves in lines, about 2.5 cm (1 inch) apart, on the dampened half of the dough strip. Fold the other half on top.

Line up parsley leaves neatly on dough so that you will be able to cut between them easily

Position dough carefully over parsley leaves so they are not dislodged

5 Roll very gently with the rolling pin to seal the dough together. Alternatively, roll the dough through the pasta machine on the second narrowest setting to seal. Prepare the remaining dough in the same way.

Flour tea towel so pasta squares do not stick

Lay pasta squares on towel in one layer, not overlapping, so they dry evenly

6 Using the fluted pasta wheel, or the chef's knife, cut the dough into roughly 2.5 cm (1 inch) squares, cutting between the parsley so that each square contains a leaf silhouette.

7 Put the squares on the floured tea towel, sprinkle them with a little flour or fine cornmeal, and allow to dry, 1-2 hours.

2 MAKE THE DRESSING AND PREPARE THE DECORATION

1 Chop the shallots. Chop the garlic. Chop the parsley.

Whisk briskly so ingredients thicken

2 In a large bowl, whisk together the vinegar, soured cream, shallots, garlic, parsley, salt and pepper until slightly thickened.

3 Gradually whisk in the oil so the dressing remains emulsified and slightly thick. Taste it for seasoning.

Keep whisking as you add oil so that it becomes fully absorbed into dressing

4 Hard-boil and shell the eggs (see box, below). With the chef's knife, cut the eggs crosswise into neat slices for decoration.

HOW TO HARD-BOIL AND SHELL EGGS

1 Put the eggs in a medium saucepan of cold water. Bring the water to the boil and simmer the eggs 10 minutes.

2 Remove the pan from the heat and immediately run cold water into the pan to stop the eggs cooking, then allow the eggs to cool in the water.

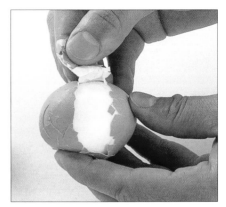

3 Drain the eggs. Tap gently to crack the shells all over, then remove the shells. Rinse the eggs, and dry with kitchen paper.

3 COOK THE PARSLEY SQUARES AND FINISH THE DISH

1 Fill the large pan with water, bring to the boil and add 15 ml (1 tbsp) salt. Add the squares and simmer until tender but still chewy, 3-5 minutes, stirring occasionally to prevent sticking.

2 Drain the parsley squares in the colander, rinse with hot water to wash away the starch, and drain again thoroughly.

3 Add the hot parsley squares to the bowl of dressing and toss gently to mix using the rubber spatula.

🍴 TO SERVE
Pile the squares on individual plates and decorate the top of the salad with slices of hard-boiled egg and a fresh parsley sprig.

Delicate parsley-patterned squares are a simple but eye-catching idea

VARIATION

PARSLEY SQUARES IN BROTH

Here, mini parsley pasta squares make an elegant garnish for a clear soup.

1 Make the parsley pasta squares as directed, using small parsley leaves and cutting the squares as small as possible.
2 Omit the dressing and hard-boiled egg decoration.
3 Bring 2 litres (3½ pints) chicken stock to the boil.
4 Meanwhile, cook and drain the parsley squares.
5 Put the parsley squares into warmed individual bowls. Spoon the hot stock over the pasta and serve at once.

— GETTING AHEAD —
The pasta squares can be made, dried and stored, loosely wrapped, in the refrigerator up to 48 hours, or they can be frozen. Sprinkle the squares lightly with flour or fine cornmeal so they do not stick together. The dressing can be made up to 24 hours ahead and kept at room temperature. The pasta should be cooked just before serving.

SPINACH AND CHEESE PINWHEELS ON PEPPER SAUCE

¶Ⓞ¶ SERVES 6 AS A MAIN COURSE ⏥ WORK TIME 35-45 MINUTES* ♨ COOKING TIME 35-40 MINUTES

EQUIPMENT

- chef's knife
- small knife
- fork
- bowls
- wooden spoon
- palette knife
- metal skewer
- table knife
- sieve
- pasta machine
- tea towels
- slotted spatula
- saucepans
- large wide pan
- frying pan
- shallow baking dish
- plastic bag
- food processor
- aluminium foil

Pasta takes on a new look when shaped as spiral pinwheels with a spinach and cheese filling and sliced to serve on a striking red pepper sauce.

* *plus 2-3 hours standing and drying time*

metric	SHOPPING LIST	imperial
	For the pasta dough	
300 g	strong plain flour, more if needed	10 oz
3	eggs	3
15 ml	vegetable oil	1 tbsp
5 ml	salt	1 tsp
	For the spinach filling	
450 g	frozen leaf spinach	15 oz
250 g	fresh goat cheese	8 oz
30 g	butter, plus extra for baking dish	1 oz
250 g	ricotta cheese	8 oz
	ground nutmeg	
	salt and pepper	
2	eggs	2
	For the topping	
60 g	butter	2 oz
60 ml	double cream	4 tbsp
	For the red pepper sauce	
1	garlic clove	1
2	spring onions	2
750 g	red peppers	1½ lb
500 g	tomatoes	1 lb
1	small bunch of fresh basil	1
30 ml	olive oil	2 tbsp

INGREDIENTS

- ricotta cheese
- eggs
- goat cheese
- vegetable oil
- red peppers
- tomatoes
- butter
- fresh basil
- olive oil
- double cream
- garlic clove
- frozen leaf spinach
- ground nutmeg
- flour
- spring onions

ORDER OF WORK

1 MAKE THE PASTA RECTANGLES

2 MAKE THE SPINACH FILLING

3 FILL, SHAPE AND BAKE THE PASTA ROLLS

4 MAKE THE RED PEPPER SAUCE

1 MAKE THE PASTA RECTANGLES

1 Make the pasta dough (see page 15). Knead and roll out the dough using the pasta machine (see pages 11-12), ending with the rollers at the second narrowest setting. Alternatively, knead and roll out the dough by hand (see pages 16-17), rolling it out in strips about 13 cm (5 inches) wide and the thickness of a table knife blade. Allow the dough to dry until it has a leathery look, 5-10 minutes.

2 With the chef's knife, trim the dough to make strips about 10 cm (4 inches) wide. Cut each strip across into rectangles 20 cm (8 inches) long, discarding the end pieces. There should be about 12 rectangles.

3 Spread out the rectangles on a floured tea towel and sprinkle them with a little flour or fine cornmeal. Allow to dry, 1-2 hours.

2 MAKE THE SPINACH FILLING

1 Cook the spinach according to package directions, then drain well and squeeze dry. Chop it finely. Crumble the goat cheese, discarding any rind.

2 Heat the butter in the frying pan, add the spinach and cook, stirring constantly, until all the moisture has evaporated, 2-3 minutes.

Beaten eggs will blend into spinach mixture evenly

3 Remove from the heat and allow to cool slightly, then stir in the ricotta and goat cheeses, a pinch of nutmeg, salt and pepper. Taste for seasoning.

4 Lightly beat the eggs to mix, then add them to the spinach mixture and stir well.

3 FILL, SHAPE AND BAKE THE PASTA ROLLS

1 Fill the large wide pan with water, bring to the boil and add 15 ml (1 tbsp) salt. Add the pasta rectangles a few at a time, and simmer until barely tender, 3-5 minutes. Stir gently from time to time to prevent sticking. As the pasta rectangles are cooked, lift them out with the slotted spatula and place in a bowl of cold water. Then drain and spread them out on a clean tea towel to drain thoroughly.

ANNE SAYS
'*Adding a little oil to the cooking water will help prevent the pasta rectangles sticking together.*'

2 Butter the baking dish. Heat the oven to 190°C (375°F, Gas 5). Using the palette knife, spread 45-60 ml (3-4 tbsp) of the spinach filling on each rectangle of dough, leaving a 5 mm (¼ inch) border.

3 Roll up the rectangles of dough from a short end into neat cylinders and arrange them in the buttered baking dish.

Roll up pasta rectangles without squeezing

4 For the topping, melt the butter and mix with the double cream. Pour over the rolls. Cover the baking dish tightly with buttered foil and bake the rolls until the skewer inserted in the centre is hot to the touch when withdrawn, about 30 minutes. While the rolls are baking, make the sauce.

HOW TO ROAST, PEEL AND CHOP A RED PEPPER

Grilling peppers makes them easy to peel, and smoky-flavoured.

1 Heat the grill. Set the whole pepper on the rack about 10 cm (4 inches) from the heat and grill it, turning as needed, until the skin is black and blistered, 10-12 minutes. Immediately put the pepper in a plastic bag, close it and leave until it is cool enough to handle (the steam trapped in the bag helps loosen the skin). With a table knife, peel off the skin.

2 Cut around the pepper core and pull it out. Halve the pepper and scrape away the seeds. Rinse the pepper under running water and pat dry.

3 Cut each pepper half into strips, then chop the strips across into chunks.

4 MAKE THE RED PEPPER SAUCE

1 Chop the garlic. Chop the spring onions. Roast, peel and chop the red peppers (see box, page 54). Peel, seed and chop the tomatoes. Discard the basil stalks and chop the leaves; keep 4-6 sprigs for decoration.

2 Heat the olive oil in the frying pan. Add the peppers, tomatoes, garlic, spring onions and chopped basil and cook, stirring occasionally, until thickened, 15-20 minutes.

3 Purée the sauce in the food processor (or in a blender) until almost smooth (small chunks of tomato and pepper add agreeable texture). Season the sauce to taste with salt and pepper.

†◯† TO SERVE Cut each roll into 2.5 cm (1 inch) slices on the diagonal, discarding the ends. Reheat the sauce and spoon a little on individual plates. Arrange 8 pinwheels on top and decorate with the reserved basil sprigs. Serve the remaining sauce separately.

VARIATION

SPINACH AND CHEESE PINWHEELS ON PARSLEY SAUCE

1 Prepare and bake the pasta as directed.
2 Meanwhile, make the parsley sauce: bring a medium pan of salted water to the boil, add 125 g (4 oz) parsley leaves and boil to blanch 1 minute. Drain the parsley in a colander, rinse under cold water and drain again thoroughly.
3 Purée the parsley in a food processor with 125 ml (4 fl oz) double cream. Pour the sauce into a small saucepan and thin it with 250 ml (8 fl oz) more cream. Heat the sauce gently and season.
4 Finish the dish as directed, arranging the pinwheels in a diagonal pattern across individual plates. Decorate with parsley leaves.

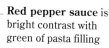

Red pepper sauce is bright contrast with green of pasta filling

GETTING AHEAD

The rolls can be prepared ready for baking and kept, covered, in the refrigerator up to 24 hours, or they can be frozen. The sauce can be made a day ahead, covered and refrigerated, but it will lose some of its fresh flavour.

Hazelnut Ravioli with Gorgonzola Sauce

 Serves 8-10   Work Time 50-60 minutes*   Cooking Time 4-5 minutes

EQUIPMENT

food processor

colander

teaspoons

pastry brush

chef's knife

baking sheet

pasta machine

fluted pasta wheel

bowls

palette knife

wooden spoons

cheese grater

chopping board

large pan

sieve

tea towels

medium saucepan

This recipe is a modern variation of an old theme. Toasted hazelnuts are ground, combined with cream cheese and served in a piquant Gorgonzola sauce. Given the intensity of flavour, they are best served as an appetiser.

* plus 2-3 hours standing and drying time

INGREDIENTS

hazelnuts

garlic cloves

eggs

cream cheese

Gorgonzola cheese

flour

butter

double cream

vegetable oil

Parmesan cheese

metric	SHOPPING LIST	imperial
	For the hazelnut filling	
210 g	hazelnuts	7 oz
60 g	Gorgonzola cheese	2 oz
2	garlic cloves	2
250 g	cream cheese	8 oz
30-45 ml	double cream	2-3 tbsp
45 ml	grated Parmesan cheese	3 tbsp
	salt and pepper	
	For the pasta dough	
300 g	strong plain flour, more if needed	10 oz
3	eggs	3
15 ml	vegetable oil	1 tbsp
5 ml	salt	1 tsp
	For the Gorgonzola sauce	
175 g	Gorgonzola cheese	6 oz
45 g	butter	1 ½ oz
125 ml	double cream	4 fl oz
	Parmesan cheese, for serving	

ORDER OF WORK

1 MAKE THE HAZELNUT FILLING

2 MAKE THE PASTA DOUGH; FILL AND CUT THE RAVIOLI

3 MAKE THE GORGONZOLA SAUCE

4 COOK THE RAVIOLI AND FINISH THE DISH

1 MAKE THE HAZELNUT FILLING

1 Heat the oven to 180°C (350°F, Gas 4). Spread the hazelnuts on the baking sheet and toast in the heated oven until lightly browned, 12-15 minutes.

ANNE SAYS

'Sprinkling the nuts with water before toasting makes removing the skins easier.'

Toasting hazelnuts makes them crisp and intensely flavoured

2 Rub the hot nuts in a rough tea towel to remove as much of the skins as possible. Grind the nuts to a coarse powder in the food processor or a blender. Transfer them to a bowl and set aside.

ANNE SAYS

'You can replace all or part of the hazelnuts with an equal quantity of walnuts. The walnuts will not need to be toasted and peeled. Simply grind them and continue with the filling as directed.'

Stir ingredients together thoroughly to combine them evenly

3 Chop the Gorgonzola cheese, discarding any rind. Chop the garlic.

ANNE SAYS

'Try to find authentic Italian Gorgonzola, because its rich creaminess gives the sauce a luxurious texture that can't be equalled.'

4 In a medium bowl, beat the cream cheese with the cream until smooth, using the wooden spoon.

5 Add the garlic, Gorgonzola and Parmesan cheeses, and the hazelnuts. Stir to mix, then season with salt and pepper.

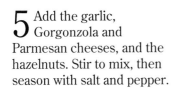

2 MAKE THE PASTA DOUGH; FILL AND CUT THE RAVIOLI

Pasta wheel gives attractive fluted edges

1 Make the pasta dough (see page 15). Knead and roll out one-quarter of the dough using the pasta machine (see pages 11-12), ending with the rollers at the narrowest setting. Alternatively, knead and roll out one-quarter of the dough by hand (see pages 16-17), rolling it out in a strip about the thickness of a postcard. Using a ruler as a guide, trim the strip of dough to a width of about 12.5 cm (5 inches), discarding the end pieces and rough edges. Cut the strip across in half. Brush one rectangle of dough very lightly with water.

ANNE SAYS
'Make the ravioli using one-quarter of the dough at a time to ensure that the dough remains moist and easy to work with.'

Press gently to seal layers of dough together

2 Using 2 teaspoons, arrange mounds of the hazelnut filling on the moistened dough, spacing them about 4 cm (1½ inches) apart. Leave a 1 cm (½ inch) border.

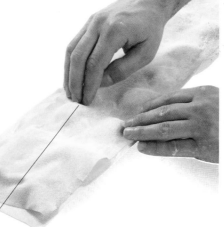

3 Lay the other rectangle of dough evenly over the filling. With your fingers, press down between the mounds of filling to seal the dough, gently pushing out any pockets of air.

4 Using the fluted pasta wheel or the chef's knife, trim the edges of the rectangle and cut between the mounds to make even 4 cm (1½ inch) squares. Roll out, fill and cut the remaining dough, using about one-quarter of the dough each time. Spread out the ravioli on a floured tea towel and sprinkle them with a little flour or fine cornmeal. Allow to dry, 1-2 hours.

ANNE SAYS
'These stuffed pastas might stick to one another or break during cooking. One way to prevent this is to freeze the ravioli before simmering. Lay them in a single layer on a floured baking sheet and freeze until solid, at least 1 hour. Cook as directed.'

3 MAKE THE GORGONZOLA SAUCE

Stir cheese constantly with wooden spoon until melted

1 Chop the Gorgonzola cheese. Melt the butter with the cream in the saucepan. Add the Gorgonzola.

2 Stir until the cheese has melted, then simmer the sauce until thickened, 5-6 minutes. The sauce should lightly coat the spoon. Season to taste with salt and pepper. Transfer the sauce to a warmed large bowl and keep warm.

4 COOK THE RAVIOLI AND FINISH THE DISH

Fold pasta and sauce together gently so pasta does not break

1 Fill the large pan with water, bring to the boil and add 15 ml (1 tbsp) salt. Add the ravioli and simmer until tender but still chewy, 4-5 minutes, stirring occasionally to prevent sticking. Drain the ravioli in the colander, rinse with hot water to wash away the starch, and drain again thoroughly.

2 Add the hot ravioli to the bowl with the Gorgonzola sauce and toss gently to coat.

🍽 TO SERVE

Arrange 5-6 ravioli on each warmed individual plate, spoon any remaining sauce over the ravioli and sprinkle with shaved curls of Parmesan cheese.

Parmesan cheese is 'shaved' into thin curls with potato or vegetable peeler

V A R I A T I O N

HAZELNUT RAVIOLI SOFFRITO

Soffrito refers to a classic Italian garnish of aromatic vegetables sautéed in olive oil. It marries well with the nutty filling of the ravioli here.

1 Prepare the hazelnut ravioli as directed.
2 Trim and finely chop 3 celery sticks. Finely chop 3 carrots. Finely chop 1 medium onion. Chop a small bunch of parsley .
3 In a medium sauté pan, heat 45-60 ml (3-4 tbsp) olive oil. Add the vegetables and cook, stirring, until they are tender but still firm, 5-8 minutes.
4 Stir in the parsley and salt and pepper to taste. Keep the soffrito warm.
5 Cook and drain the ravioli as directed.
6 Arrange the ravioli on warmed individual plates and spoon the soffrito on top. Serve immediately.

GETTING AHEAD

The ravioli can be made, dried and stored, loosely wrapped, in the refrigerator up to 24 hours, or they can be frozen. Sprinkle them lightly with flour or fine cornmeal so that the pieces do not stick together.
Cook the ravioli and make the Gorgonzola sauce just before serving.

CHINESE HALF MOONS WITH LEMON SAUCE

🍽 SERVES 8-10 AS AN APPETISER 🥣 WORK TIME 45-50 MINUTES* 🍲 COOKING TIME 2-3 MINUTES

EQUIPMENT

food processor

colander

chef's knife

pastry brush

teaspoon

wooden spoon

palette knife

bowls

grater

frying pan

kitchen paper

plate

large pan

pasta machine

sieve

saucepans

7.5 cm (3 inch) pastry cutter

A filling of chopped prawns and Chinese leaves gives texture to these pasta turnovers, served in a tangy lemon sauce. Chinese leaves add an oriental touch, but white cabbage does well, too.

*plus 2-3 hours standing and drying time

metric	SHOPPING LIST	imperial
	For the filling	
175 g	peeled cooked prawns	6 oz
125 g	Chinese leaves	4 oz
1	small spring onion	1
1	garlic clove	1
1	shallot	1
2.5 cm	piece of fresh root ginger	1 inch
1	lemon	1
15 ml	vegetable oil	1 tbsp
	pepper	
5 ml	sherry	1 tsp
15 ml	soy sauce	1 tbsp
	For the pasta dough	
300 g	strong plain flour, more if needed	10 oz
3	eggs	3
15 ml	vegetable oil	1 tbsp
5 ml	salt	1 tsp
	For the lemon sauce	
1	spring onion	1
2	lemons	2
45 g	butter	1½ oz
75 ml	double cream	2½ fl oz

INGREDIENTS

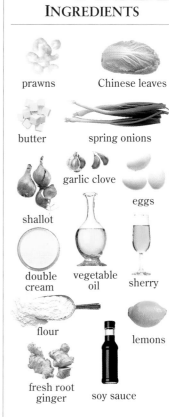

prawns

Chinese leaves

butter

spring onions

garlic clove

eggs

shallot

double cream

vegetable oil

sherry

flour

lemons

fresh root ginger

soy sauce

ORDER OF WORK

1 PREPARE THE INGREDIENTS FOR THE FILLING

2 COOK THE FILLING

3 MAKE THE PASTA DOUGH; FILL AND SHAPE THE HALF MOONS

4 MAKE THE SAUCE AND COOK THE HALF MOONS

1 PREPARE THE INGREDIENTS FOR THE FILLING

1 If using frozen prawns, thaw them, then dry them on kitchen paper. Coarsely chop the prawns.

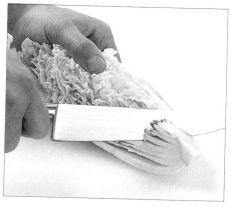

2 Slice away the core of the Chinese leaves and discard it. Cut the leaves crosswise into very fine shreds. After shredding, discard any thick ribs, then rinse the leaves under running water.

Rinse shredded Chinese leaves in colander so they can be tipped easily into pan of boiling water

Chinese leaves will wilt and soften when added to boiling water

3 Bring a pan of salted water to the boil, add the shredded leaves and simmer until just tender, 3-5 minutes. Drain in the colander, rinse with cold water and drain thoroughly.

4 Chop the spring onion. Chop the garlic. Chop the shallot. Peel and finely chop the root ginger.

Rub lemon on fine grid of grater to remove zest without any bitter white pith

5 Grate the zest from the lemon on to the plate.

2 COOK THE FILLING

Be sure frying pan is large enough to contain all ingredients

1 Heat the oil in the frying pan, add the Chinese leaves, spring onion, garlic, shallot, ginger and pepper and sauté, stirring, about 3 minutes. Add the prawns, lemon zest, sherry and soy sauce and stir well. Taste the filling for seasoning.

2 Coarsely chop the filling in the food processor. Alternatively, finely chop the filling by hand.

! TAKE CARE !
If using the food processor, do not purée the filling too finely.

3 MAKE THE PASTA DOUGH; FILL AND SHAPE THE HALF MOONS

1 Make the pasta dough (see page 15). Knead and roll out one-quarter of the dough using the pasta machine (see pages 11-12), ending with the rollers at the narrowest setting. Alternatively, knead and roll out one-quarter of the dough by hand (see pages 16-17), rolling it out in a strip about the thickness of a postcard.

2 Lay the strip of dough on the work surface. Using the pastry cutter or a sharp-edged glass, cut out a round from the dough. Spoon about 5 ml (1 tsp) of filling on to the centre of the round. Using the pastry brush or your finger, brush the edge of the dough round lightly with water.

3 Fold one side of the pasta round over the other to enclose the filling, then seal it by pinching the edges together with your fingers.

! TAKE CARE !
Be sure to pinch carefully to keep the edges from opening during cooking.

4 Cut, fill and seal the rest of the strip of dough, then continue with the remaining dough to make more half moons, kneading and rolling out about one-quarter of the dough each time. Spread out the half moons on the floured tea towel and sprinkle generously with flour or fine cornmeal. Allow to dry, 1-2 hours.

4 MAKE THE SAUCE AND COOK THE HALF MOONS

Lemon zest is grated finely so sauce will be smooth

1 Make the lemon sauce: with the chef's knife, finely slice the green part of the spring onion; set aside for the garnish. Grate the zest from the lemons, using the finest side of the grater.

Half moons make an unusual appetiser, or serve them as a main course for 6 with stir-fried vegetables

2 Melt the butter in a small saucepan, then stir in the cream and half of the lemon zest. Keep warm.

3 Fill the large pan with water, bring to the boil and add 15 ml (1 tbsp) salt. Add the half moons and cook until tender but still chewy, 2-3 minutes, stirring occasionally to prevent sticking. Drain the half moons in the colander, rinse with hot water to wash away the starch, and drain again thoroughly.

ANNE SAYS
'*These stuffed pastas can be delicate to work with, because they tend to stick to one another or break during cooking. One way to ensure success is to freeze the half moons before cooking. Lay them in a single layer on a floured baking sheet and freeze until solid, at least 1 hour. Cook as directed.*'

¶❂¶ TO SERVE
Arrange the half moons on warmed individual plates. Spoon the lemon sauce over the pasta and sprinkle with the sliced spring onion and reserved lemon zest.

—— GETTING AHEAD ——
The half moons can be made, dried and stored, loosely wrapped, in the refrigerator up to 24 hours, or they can be frozen. Sprinkle them lightly with flour or fine cornmeal so that the pieces do not stick together. Cook the half moons and make the sauce just before serving.

CRAB RAVIOLI WITH SAFFRON BUTTER SAUCE

 SERVES 6 OR 8   WORK TIME 40-50 MINUTES*   COOKING TIME 8-10 MINUTES

EQUIPMENT

pasta machine**

sieve

palette knife

chef's knife

chopping board

medium saucepan

pastry brush

tea towel

fluted pasta wheel

colander

bowls

whisk

teaspoon

large pan

metal spoon

wooden spoon

**rolling pin can also be used

ANNE SAYS

'Saffron threads are stamens of a species of crocus; a pinch colours and flavours a dish.'

Twenty years ago, if you said 'ravioli', everyone imagined meat-filled squares in tomato sauce. In this contemporary recipe, ravioli are filled with crab and served with a rich saffron butter sauce.

GETTING AHEAD

The ravioli can be made, dried and stored, loosely wrapped, in the refrigerator up to 24 hours, or they can be frozen. Sprinkle them lightly with flour or fine cornmeal so that the pieces do not stick together. Simmer the ravioli and make the saffron butter sauce just before serving.

* plus 2-3 hours standing and drying time

INGREDIENTS

white crabmeat

ricotta cheese   eggs

saffron threads   flour

spring onions

white wine

shallots

vegetable oil   butter

double cream

metric	SHOPPING LIST	imperial
	For the filling	
375 g	cooked fresh or canned white crabmeat	12 oz
3	spring onions	3
90 g	ricotta cheese	3 oz
	salt and white pepper	
	For the pasta dough	
300 g	strong plain flour, more if needed	10 oz
3	eggs	3
15 ml	vegetable oil	1 tbsp
5 ml	salt	1 tsp
	For the saffron butter sauce	
	saffron threads	
45-60 ml	boiling water	3-4 tbsp
250 g	cold unsalted butter	8 oz
2	shallots	2
45 ml	dry white wine	3 tbsp
15 ml	double cream	1 tbsp

ORDER OF WORK

1 **MAKE THE CRAB FILLING**

2 **MAKE THE PASTA DOUGH; FILL AND CUT THE RAVIOLI**

3 **MAKE THE SAFFRON BUTTER SAUCE**

4 **COOK THE CRAB RAVIOLI**

1 MAKE THE CRAB FILLING

1 Drain the crabmeat if necessary. Using your fingers, coarsely shred the crabmeat, discarding any membrane, and put it in a bowl.

2 With the chef's knife, trim the ends of the spring onions. Finely chop the white and green parts.

3 Add half of the spring onions and the ricotta to the crabmeat and season to taste with salt and pepper. Stir to mix. Reserve the remaining onions for sprinkling at the end.

2 MAKE THE PASTA DOUGH; FILL AND CUT THE RAVIOLI

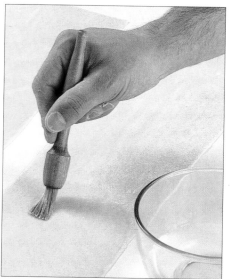

1 Make the pasta dough (see page 15). Knead and roll out one-quarter of the dough using the pasta machine (see pages 11-12), ending with the rollers at the narrowest setting. Alternatively, knead and roll out one-quarter of the dough by hand (see pages 16-17), rolling it out in a strip about the thickness of a postcard. Using a ruler as a guide, trim the strip of dough to a width of about 13 cm (5 inches), discarding the end pieces and rough edges. Cut the strip across in half. Brush one rectangle of dough very lightly with water.

2 Using the teaspoon, arrange small mounds of the crab filling on the moistened dough, spacing them about 5 cm (2 inches) apart. Leave a 1 cm (½ inch) border.

ANNE SAYS
'Make the ravioli using one-quarter of the dough at a time to ensure that the dough remains moist and easy to work with.'

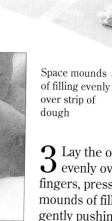

Space mounds of filling evenly over strip of dough

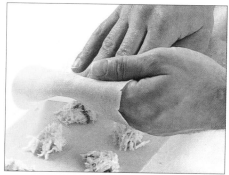

3 Lay the other rectangle of dough evenly over the filling. With your fingers, press down between the mounds of filling to seal the dough, gently pushing out any pockets of air.

4 Using the fluted pasta wheel or the chef's knife, trim the edges of the rectangle and cut between the mounds to make even 4 cm (1½ inch) squares. Roll out, fill and cut the remaining dough, using about one-quarter of the dough each time.

ANNE SAYS
'*These ravioli can also be cut into giant 10 cm (4 inch) squares.*'

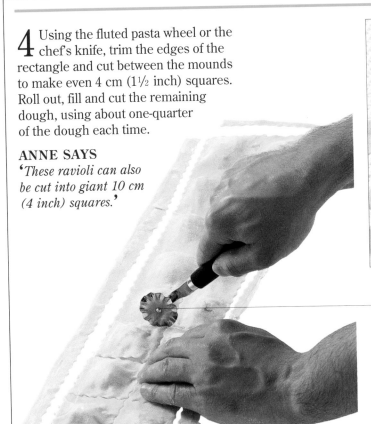

Rolling pasta wheel cuts out ravioli easily and neatly

Ravioli will have decorative edges if you use floured pasta wheel

5 Spread out the ravioli on the floured tea towel and sprinkle them with a little flour or fine cornmeal. Allow to dry, 1-2 hours.

ANNE SAYS
'*These stuffed pastas can be delicate to work with, because they might stick to one another or break during cooking. One way to prevent this is to freeze the ravioli before simmering. Lay them in a single layer on a floured baking sheet and freeze until solid, at least 1 hour. Cook as directed.*'

3 MAKE THE SAFFRON BUTTER SAUCE

1 Put a large pinch of saffron threads in a small bowl, add the boiling water and stir well to mix. Leave to soak 10 minutes. Meanwhile, cut the butter into small pieces and chill in the refrigerator. Finely chop the shallots.

2 Put the wine in the medium saucepan, add the soaked saffron with its liquid and the chopped shallots and stir to combine. Boil the mixture 2-3 minutes to a syrupy glaze; add the cream and boil again to a glaze.

3 Take the saucepan from the heat and whisk in the butter, a little at a time, whisking constantly and moving the pan on and off the heat. The butter should thicken the sauce creamily but without melting to oil. Take care not to let the sauce get too hot or it will separate. Season to taste with salt and white pepper.

4 COOK THE CRAB RAVIOLI

1 Fill the large pan with water, bring to the boil and add 15 ml (1 tbsp) salt. Add the ravioli and simmer until tender but still chewy, 4-5 minutes, stirring occasionally with the wooden spoon to prevent sticking.

ANNE SAYS
'While the ravioli is cooking, the sauce can be kept warm up to 15 minutes: set the saucepan on a rack in a pan of warm, not hot, water. Whisk the sauce occasionally.'

2 Drain the ravioli in the colander, rinse gently with hot water to wash away the starch and drain again thoroughly.

🍴 TO SERVE
Put the ravioli on warmed individual plates, slightly overlapping them. Spoon the saffron butter sauce over the ravioli, sprinkle with the reserved spring onions and serve immediately.

LOBSTER RAVIOLI WITH SAFFRON BUTTER SAUCE

In this elegant variation of crab ravioli, the crabmeat is replaced with lobster tail cut into thin medallions.

1 Cut a 375 g (12 oz) cooked lobster tail into thin medallions. Reserve 6 large medallions for garnish and chop the remaining lobster. Mix it with the spring onions, ricotta, salt and pepper.
2 Make the pasta dough and fill and cook the ravioli as directed.
3 For presentation, spoon the saffron butter sauce on to warmed individual plates, then lay the ravioli on the sauce so that their tips meet in the centre. Set a lobster medallion in the centre.

Spring onion garnish gives bright green colour contrast as well as mild oniony crunch

CHEESE TORTELLINI WITH SMOKED SALMON AND DILL

 SERVES 6 OR 8 WORK TIME 55-65 MINUTES* 🍲 COOKING TIME 3-5 MINUTES

EQUIPMENT

pasta machine**

teaspoon

pastry brush

chef's knife

fork

colander

cheese grater

large pan

palette knife

wooden spoon

large saucepan

tea towel

bowls

sieve

chopping board

6 cm (2½ inch)
pastry cutter

** rolling pin can also be used

These tortellini are filled with a mixture of cheeses and served with smoked salmon strips and fresh sprigs of dill bound lightly with cream.

GETTING AHEAD

The tortellini can be made, dried and stored, loosely wrapped, in the refrigerator up to 24 hours. Sprinkle them lightly with flour or fine cornmeal so that the pieces do not stick together. Cook the tortellini just before serving.

* plus 2-3 hours standing and drying time

metric	SHOPPING LIST	imperial
	For the filling	
150 g	mozzarella cheese	5 oz
300 g	ricotta cheese	10 oz
30 g	grated Parmesan cheese	1 oz
	ground nutmeg	
	salt and pepper	
1	egg	1
	For the topping	
125 g	smoked salmon	4 oz
1	small bunch of fresh dill	1
60 g	butter	2 oz
250 ml	double cream	8 fl oz
	For the pasta dough	
300 g	strong plain flour, more if needed	10 oz
3	eggs	3
15 ml	vegetable oil	1 tbsp
5 ml	salt	1 tsp

INGREDIENTS

Parmesan cheese

mozzarella cheese

double cream

eggs

vegetable oil

butter

ricotta cheese

ground nutmeg

fresh dill

flour

smoked salmon

ORDER OF WORK

1 PREPARE THE FILLING AND TOPPING

2 MAKE THE PASTA DOUGH; FILL AND SHAPE THE TORTELLINI

3 COOK THE TORTELLINI AND FINISH THE DISH

1 PREPARE THE FILLING AND TOPPING

1 Cut the mozzarella into small cubes and put them in a large bowl. Add the ricotta and the Parmesan and mix with the wooden spoon. Add a pinch of nutmeg and salt and pepper to taste.

2 Lightly beat the egg with the fork, then mix into the filling to bind it.

3 Cut the smoked salmon into strips. Chop the dill, reserving a pretty sprig for garnish.

2 MAKE THE PASTA DOUGH; FILL AND SHAPE THE TORTELLINI

1 Make the pasta dough (see page 15). Knead and roll out one-quarter of the dough using the pasta machine (see pages 11-12), ending with the rollers at the narrowest setting. Alternatively, knead and roll out one-quarter of the dough by hand (see pages 16-17), rolling it out in a strip about the thickness of a postcard.

Roll out only one-quarter of dough at a time so it remains moist and easy to work with

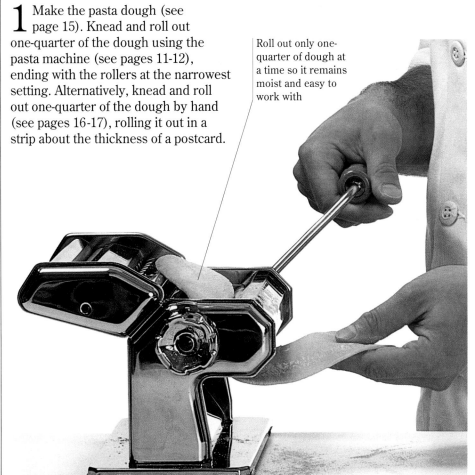

2 Lay the strip of dough on the work surface. Using the pastry cutter, cut out rounds from the dough.

ANNE SAYS
'You can also use a sharp-edged glass to cut out the pasta rounds.'

3 Using the pastry brush or your finger, brush the edge of one dough round lightly with water. Spoon about 5 ml (1 tsp) of filling on to the centre of the round.

Household teaspoon holds just right amount of filling

4 Holding the dough round in the palm of your hand, fold one side of the pasta over the other to enclose the filling, then seal it by pinching the edges together with your fingers.

! TAKE CARE !
Be sure to pinch well to prevent the edges from opening during cooking.

5 Curve the dough around your finger, turning the sealed edge up at the same time to form a curved upward pleat. Pinch the pointed ends together to form a ring.

6 Fill and shape the remaining dough rounds. Roll out, cut and fill the remaining dough in the same way, using about one-quarter of the dough at a time. Spread out the tortellini on the floured tea towel and sprinkle generously with flour or fine cornmeal. Allow to dry, 1-2 hours.

3 COOK THE TORTELLINI AND FINISH THE DISH

1 Fill the large pan with water, bring to the boil and add 15 ml (1 tbsp) salt. Add the tortellini and simmer until tender but still chewy, 3-5 minutes, stirring occasionally to prevent sticking. Drain in the colander, rinse with hot water to wash away the starch, and drain again thoroughly.

2 Melt the butter in the saucepan. Add the drained tortellini and toss them gently with the wooden spoon until they are all warm and evenly coated with melted butter.

3 Add the smoked salmon, chopped dill and cream. Toss over moderate heat until thoroughly heated.

🍴 **TO SERVE**
Transfer the tortellini to a warmed platter or individual plates and garnish with the reserved dill.

Fresh green herb garnish
is ideal for a creamy dish,
and dill has an affinity
with salmon

V A R I A T I O N S

CHEESE TORTELLINI WITH PEAS

1 Simmer 60 g (2 oz) frozen green peas in boiling salted water until just tender, then drain thoroughly.
2 Follow the recipe as directed, and add the peas to the tortellini with the salmon, dill and cream.

CHEESE TORTELLINI WITH RED PEPPER SAUCE

1 Omit the smoked salmon, cream, butter and dill.
2 Make the tortellini as directed.
3 Make a red pepper sauce (see Spinach and Cheese Pinwheels, page 55).
4 Cook and drain the tortellini.
5 Toss the tortellini and sauce together over moderate heat until thoroughly heated and transfer to individual plates.
6 Garnish with sprigs of fresh basil, if you like.

MARIA'S TORTELLINI

 SERVES 4 OR 6-8 WORK TIME 65-75 MINUTES* ▦ COOKING TIME 10-15 MINUTES

EQUIPMENT

bowls

chopping board

fork

pastry brush

chef's knife

frying pan

large pan

meat mincer

palette knife

colander

wooden spoon

pasta machine

cheese grater

tea towel

kitchen paper

large saucepan

pastry cutter

sieve

Tortellini translates literally as 'small pies', though legend has it they were shaped to resemble Venus' navel by an innkeeper who spied on her through a keyhole. Flavours vary widely; these tortellini have a stuffing of minced meats and are topped with butter and cheese. This recipe is time-consuming, but the result is worth it.

* plus 2-3 hours standing and drying time

INGREDIENTS

lean boneless pork

mortadella

eggs

boneless chicken breast

Parma ham

Parmesan cheese

butter

flour

vegetable oil

ground nutmeg

metric	SHOPPING LIST	imperial
	For the meat filling	
90 g	skinless, boneless chicken breast	3 oz
90 g	lean boneless pork	3 oz
30 g	butter	1 oz
2	slices of Parma ham	2
2	slices of mortadella	2
60 g	grated Parmesan cheese	2 oz
	ground nutmeg	
	salt and pepper	
1	egg	1
	For the pasta dough	
300 g	strong plain flour, more if needed	10 oz
3	eggs	3
15 ml	vegetable oil	1 tbsp
5 ml	salt	1 tsp
	To finish	
60 g	butter	2 oz
30 g	grated Parmesan cheese	1 oz

ORDER OF WORK

1 MAKE THE MEAT FILLING

2 MAKE THE PASTA DOUGH; FILL AND SHAPE THE TORTELLINI

3 COOK THE TORTELLINI AND FINISH THE DISH

1 MAKE THE MEAT FILLING

Turn pieces of chicken and pork so they seal on all sides

Cook meats briefly without browning them

1 Cut the chicken and pork into medium dice.

2 Heat the butter in the frying pan, add the chicken and pork and sauté, stirring occasionally, until they are lightly cooked but not brown, about 5 minutes. Drain the meats on kitchen paper.

3 Cut each slice of Parma ham and mortadella into 2-3 pieces.

Mince meats finely for smooth-textured filling

4 Work the chicken, pork, Parma ham and mortadella through the fine blade of the mincer or in a food processor.

ANNE SAYS
'*A mincer gives the filling a lighter texture. If you use a food processor, do not purée the meat too finely. For a filling with slightly more texture, chop the cooked pork and chicken by hand with the Parma ham and mortadella instead of mincing them.*'

5 Transfer the minced meats to a large bowl and add the cheese, a pinch of nutmeg, salt and plenty of pepper. Taste the mixture (it should be highly seasoned). Lightly beat the egg with the fork, then stir it in.

ANNE SAYS
'*Taste the mixture for seasoning before adding the raw egg.*'

2 MAKE THE PASTA DOUGH; FILL AND SHAPE THE TORTELLINI

1 Make the pasta dough (see page 15). Knead and roll out one-quarter of the dough using the pasta machine (see pages 11-12), ending with the rollers at the narrowest setting. Alternatively, knead and roll out one-quarter of the dough by hand (see pages 16-17), rolling it out in a strip to about the thickness of a postcard. Cut out rounds with a 6 cm (2 ½ inch) pastry cutter.

ANNE SAYS
'Use one-quarter of the dough at a time to ensure the dough remains moist.'

Gently shape filling into mound

2 Using the pastry brush or your finger, brush the edge of one dough round lightly with water. Put about 5 ml (1 tsp) of filling on to the centre of the round, using your fingers if you like.

3 Holding the filled dough round in the palm of your hand, fold one side over the other to enclose the filling. Seal the dough by pinching the edges together with your fingers, then curve it around your finger, turning the sealed edge up at the same time to form an upward-curved pleat. Pinch the pointed ends together to form a ring.

! TAKE CARE !
Be sure to pinch well to prevent the tortellini from opening during cooking.

Sprinkle flour over tortellini to prevent them sticking together

4 Fill and shape the rest of the dough rounds from the strip. Roll out and fill the remaining dough, using about one-quarter of the dough each time. Spread the tortellini out on the floured tea towel, sprinkle them generously with flour or fine cornmeal, then allow the tortellini to dry, 1-2 hours.

3 COOK THE TORTELLINI AND FINISH THE DISH

If stirred gently, wooden spoon will not break up tortellini

1 Fill the large pan with water, bring to the boil and add 15 ml (1 tbsp) salt. Add the tortellini and simmer until tender but still chewy, 3-5 minutes, stirring gently from time to time to prevent the tortellini sticking together. Drain in the colander, rinse with hot water to wash away the starch and drain again thoroughly.

ANNE SAYS
'*To rinse pasta quickly, dip the colander of drained pasta into a bowl of hot water, then lift out the colander and drain again.*'

2 Melt the butter in the large saucepan, add the tortellini and toss gently over the heat to coat them.

TO SERVE
Pile the tortellini on warmed individual plates, sprinkle with the Parmesan cheese and serve.

Freshly grated Parmesan cheese is finishing touch

Plump tortellini are filled with minced pork and chicken

VARIATION

TORTELLINI WITH CARAMELISED ONIONS

An easy topping for Maria's Tortellini is sliced onions, sautéed until they are soft, brown and sweet. Omit the Parmesan cheese for finishing the dish.

1 Thinly slice 6 medium onions.
2 Heat about 60 g (2 oz) butter in a heavy-based flameproof casserole or saucepan and add the onions with a pinch of sugar, salt and pepper. Press a piece of foil on top, cover with the lid and cook very gently, stirring occasionally, 15-20 minutes.
3 Remove the lid and foil and continue cooking, stirring often, until the onions are very brown and caramelised, 5-10 minutes more.
4 Make and cook the tortellini as directed.
5 Toss the tortellini with melted butter and the caramelised onions and serve immediately.

GETTING AHEAD
The tortellini can be made, dried and stored, loosely wrapped, in the refrigerator up to 24 hours, or they can be frozen. Sprinkle them lightly with flour or fine cornmeal so that they do not stick together. Cook the tortellini and add the cheese and butter just before serving.

ALSATIAN CURLY NOODLES WITH SAUTEED CHICKEN LIVERS

Spaetzli

 SERVES 6 AS AN APPETISER   WORK TIME 30-40 MINUTES*   COOKING TIME 15-20 MINUTES

EQUIPMENT

chef's knife

small knife

frying pan   tea towels

palette knife

small saucepan

large forks   sieve

slotted spoon

small ladle

large pan

fork

bowls

wooden spoon

chopping board

INGREDIENTS

chicken livers

garlic cloves

onion

salad greens

butter   eggs

flour

Spaetzli, slightly chewy in texture and twisted in uneven curls, are the Alsatian alternative to noodles. The word spaetzli *means 'little sparrows' in German. Tender chicken livers provide a wonderful contrast to the spaetzli.*

GETTING AHEAD

The spaetzli can be cooked up to 3 hours ahead and kept in a bowl of cold water. Undercook them slightly to allow for reheating. Sauté the chicken livers and reheat the spaetzli in melted butter just before serving.

* plus 30-40 minutes chilling time

metric	SHOPPING LIST	imperial
125 g	butter	4 oz
250 g	mixed salad greens and fresh herbs	8 oz
	For the spaetzli dough	
475 g	flour	15 oz
	salt and pepper	
2	eggs	2
250 ml	water, more if needed	8 fl oz
	For the chicken livers	
250 g	chicken livers	8 oz
2	garlic cloves	2
1	medium onion	1
30 g	butter	1 oz

ORDER OF WORK

1 MAKE THE SPAETZLI DOUGH

2 SHAPE, CUT AND COOK SPAETZLI

3 SAUTE THE CHICKEN LIVERS AND FINISH THE DISH

1 MAKE THE SPAETZLI DOUGH

1 Sift the flour with 5 ml (1 tsp) salt on to the work surface.

2 Make a well in the centre of the flour with your fingers.

3 Lightly beat the eggs in a small bowl with the fork. Add the eggs and half of the water to the well.

Beat eggs to mix before adding to flour

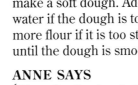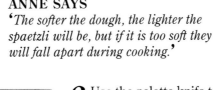

4 Mix the eggs and water together in the well with your fingers, then gradually draw the flour into the liquid mixture.

5 Continue mixing in the flour, slowly adding water as you go, to make a soft dough. Add a little more water if the dough is too dry or a little more flour if it is too sticky. Work just until the dough is smooth.

ANNE SAYS
'The softer the dough, the lighter the spaetzli will be, but if it is too soft they will fall apart during cooking.'

6 Use the palette knife to scrape up bits of dough that stick to the surface.

Fingers are best for mixing dough

7 Shape the dough into a ball, put it in a bowl and cover with a tea towel. Chill 30-40 minutes.

Push flour into dough with palette knife

2 SHAPE, CUT AND COOK SPAETZLI

1 Fill the large pan with salted water and bring almost to the boil. Meanwhile, divide the dough into 2-3 pieces with the chef's knife. On a floured surface, flatten one piece with the floured heel of your hand until it is about 5 mm (¼ inch) thick.

2 Wet the knife and cut the piece of flattened dough lengthwise in half, then cut crosswise into strips.

ANNE SAYS
'The knife should be wet to keep it from sticking to the dough.'

3 Immediately push the spaetzli into the simmering water with the knife. Simmer until they swell, rise to the surface and are almost tender, 5-7 minutes; they should have the *al dente* consistency of pasta.

ANNE SAYS
'While the first batch of spaetzli is cooking, flatten the next piece of dough and slice it, ready for cooking.'

1 Peel the onion and trim the top; leave the root intact. Cut the onion lengthwise in half and put one half, cut side down, on a chopping board. With a chef's knife, make a series of horizontal cuts from the top towards the root (but not through it).

2 Make a series of lengthwise vertical cuts in the onion half, cutting just to the root but not through it.

ANNE SAYS
'When slicing, tuck your fingertips under and use your knuckles to guide the blade of the knife.'

4 Melt the butter in the small saucepan and keep warm. When the spaetzli are cooked, lift them out with the slotted spoon and put in a warmed shallow bowl. Keep them warm while cooking the rest. Pour the melted butter over the spaetzli in the bowl and gently toss with the butter, using the large forks. Keep warm while cooking the chicken livers.

Small ladle is perfect for spooning melted butter over spaetzli

3 Slice the onion crosswise to obtain a dice (adjust the distance between slices depending on whether you want a coarse or fine dice). For finely chopped onion, continue chopping to the fineness wanted.

3 SAUTE THE CHICKEN LIVERS AND FINISH THE DISH

1 Wash the salad greens and pat dry with a tea towel. Wash the chicken livers and drain well. With the small knife, trim off any membrane or green spots and cut each liver into 2-3 pieces. Chop the garlic cloves. Chop the onion (see box, page 78).

Stir livers so they cook evenly

2 Heat the butter in the frying pan and sauté the garlic and onion until soft but not brown, 3-4 minutes, stirring with the wooden spoon. Add the chicken livers to the pan and sauté until browned on the outside but still pink in the centre, 2-3 minutes. Season with salt and pepper.

¶◉¶ TO SERVE

Gently mix the chicken livers with the warm spaetzli and spoon into individual shallow bowls. Arrange the salad greens and fresh herbs around the spaetzli.

Assorted salad leaves provide crisp, colourful contrast

Chervil sprig is delicate garnish for spaetzli

VARIATION

BUTTER-FRIED CURLY NOODLES

Plain spaetzli, browned in butter, are an excellent accompaniment to braised beef or chicken in a sauce.

1 Prepare and cook the spaetzli as directed.
2 Melt the butter in a frying pan, add the spaetzli and cook them over moderate heat, stirring, until they are browned and slightly crisp, 5-8 minutes.

ANNE SAYS
'*You might like to try plain spaetzli instead of noodles with your favourite pasta sauce.*'

SEMOLINA GNOCCHI WITH CHEESE

 SERVES 8 AS AN APPETISER   WORK TIME 30-35 MINUTES*   COOKING TIME 15-20 MINUTES

EQUIPMENT

saucepans, 1 with lid

pastry brush

fork

conical sieve

metal spoon

whisk

cheese grater

6 individual gratin dishes**

5 cm (2 inch) round pastry cutter

bowls

23 x 32.5 cm (9 x 13 inch) baking dish

wooden spoon

** other ovenproof dishes can also be used

INGREDIENTS

onion

semolina

Dijon mustard

Parmesan cheese

milk

butter

bay leaf

clove

egg yolks

ground nutmeg

black peppercorns

Made with semolina and baked with butter and cheese, these gnocchi – called gnocchi Romana *in Italian – make an excellent appetiser. They are also a traditional Roman accompaniment to braised beef. The rounds look attractive, but you can also cut squares or triangles.*

GETTING AHEAD

The gnocchi can be prepared up to 48 hours ahead and kept, covered, in the refrigerator. Add melted butter and cheese and bake just before serving.

* plus 2 hours chilling time

metric	SHOPPING LIST	imperial
	butter for dishes	
1	clove	1
1	medium onion	1
1	bay leaf	1
5 ml	black peppercorns	1 tsp
	ground nutmeg	
	salt and pepper	
1 litre	milk, more if needed	1²/₃ pints
175 g	coarse or fine semolina	6 oz
3	egg yolks	3
90 g	grated Parmesan cheese	3 oz
15 ml	Dijon mustard	1 tbsp
60 g	butter	2 oz

ORDER OF WORK

1 MAKE THE GNOCCHI MIXTURE

2 SHAPE AND BAKE THE GNOCCHI

1 MAKE THE GNOCCHI MIXTURE

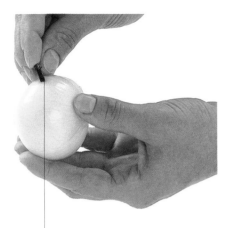

Press clove firmly into onion

1 Thickly butter the shallow flameproof baking dish. Stick the clove into the onion and put it in a medium saucepan.

2 Add the bay leaf, peppercorns, a pinch of nutmeg, a little salt and the milk to the pan. Slowly bring to the boil, then remove from the heat, cover and leave to allow the flavours to infuse, 8-12 minutes.

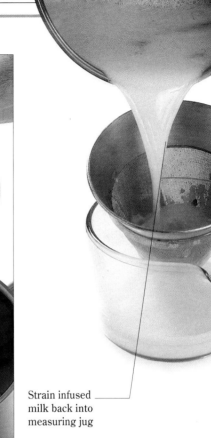

Strain infused milk back into measuring jug

3 Strain the milk and discard the flavourings. Rinse out the saucepan, return the milk to it and bring back to the boil.

4 Over moderate heat, gradually whisk the semolina into the milk in a steady stream.

ANNE SAYS
'*Whisk constantly as you add the semolina to the hot milk to keep the mixture from becoming lumpy.*'

Mixture should be thick but not stiff

5 Bring to the boil and simmer, stirring constantly with the wooden spoon, until the mixture is thick and smooth but still falls easily from the spoon, 3-5 minutes.

Mix yolks before adding
so they blend in smoothly

6 Beat the egg yolks with
the fork to mix. Remove
the pan from the heat and
gradually add the egg yolks, beating
the mixture well after each addition;
the heat of the mixture will cook and
slightly thicken the yolks.

Beat in egg yolks
gradually so they
begin to cook in heat
of mixture

7 Stir in two-thirds of the cheese and
the mustard. Add salt and pepper
to taste.

ANNE SAYS
*'The mixture should not be bland,
so season generously.'*

Small paintbrush makes
ideal 'pastry brush' for
brushing melted butter
over gnocchi mixture

8 Spoon the gnocchi mixture
into the prepared baking
dish. Using the back of the
oiled metal spoon, spread out
the gnocchi mixture to form a
1 cm (1/2 inch) layer.

Brush melted butter
over gnocchi mixture
so it will not dry out
in refrigerator

9 Melt the butter in a small pan.
Brush half of the melted butter
over the gnocchi mixture and chill in
the refrigerator until set, about 2 hours.

2 SHAPE AND BAKE THE GNOCCHI

Sprinkle Parmesan on gnocchi rounds

1 Heat the oven to 230°C (450°F, Gas 8). Warm the baking dish lightly over very gentle heat on the stove to melt the butter and loosen the gnocchi mixture. Cut out 5 cm (2 inch) rounds with the pastry cutter; discard the trimmings.

ANNE SAYS
'If you don't have a pastry cutter, you can use the top of a sharp-edged glass to cut out the rounds.'

2 Butter the gratin or other ovenproof dishes. Divide the gnocchi rounds among the dishes. Brush with the remaining melted butter and sprinkle with the remaining cheese. Bake the gnocchi until lightly browned and very hot, 15-20 minutes. Serve in the dishes.

Gnocchi rounds are rich and buttery yet light

Parmesan cheese topping toasts to an appealing golden brown

SEMOLINA GNOCCHI WITH PARMA HAM AND PINE NUTS

In this recipe, Parma ham takes the place of some of the cheese in the main recipe, while toasted pine nuts garnish the top. Serve as an appetiser or accompaniment to roast chicken.

1 Prepare the gnocchi as directed, using only half of the Parmesan cheese and adding 125 g (4 oz) chopped Parma ham to the mixture.
2 After chilling, cut the gnocchi into 16 triangles and arrange them, slightly overlapping, in a buttered large baking dish. Bake as directed.
3 Meanwhile, sprinkle 90 g (3 oz) pine nuts on a baking sheet and bake in the oven 2-3 minutes or until toasted.
4 Sprinkle the toasted pine nuts over the baked gnocchi and serve.

SPAGHETTI WITH SPRING VEGETABLES

Spaghetti Primavera

 SERVES 4 OR 6   WORK TIME 45-50 MINUTES   COOKING TIME 5-8 MINUTES

EQUIPMENT

wooden spoon

chef's knife

colander

large pan

large forks

cheese grater

chopping board   bowls

saucepans

baking sheet

aluminium foil

The green and orange of the vegetables – the younger, the better – in pasta primavera *epitomise the colours of spring. Other possible additions include bulb fennel, green pepper, mangetouts or sugar snap peas, broccoli, small French beans, baby corn-on-the-cob and asparagus tips. Delicate, finger-sized baby courgettes make a most attractive garnish.*

GETTING AHEAD

The vegetables and garnish can be prepared 2-3 hours ahead. Reheat the courgette fans in a low oven; cook the pasta and finish the sauce just before serving.

metric	SHOPPING LIST	imperial
2	medium courgettes	2
	salt and pepper	
2	medium carrots	2
210 g	shelled fresh peas	7 oz
4	baby courgettes, for garnish	4
45 g	butter + extra for baking sheet	1½ oz
500 g	spaghetti	1 lb
175 ml	double cream	6 fl oz
30 g	grated Parmesan cheese	1 oz

INGREDIENTS

spaghetti

courgettes

double cream   butter

Parmesan cheese

peas   baby courgettes

carrots

ORDER OF WORK

1 PREPARE THE VEGETABLES

2 MAKE COURGETTE GARNISH

3 COOK THE SPAGHETTI AND FINISH THE SAUCE

1 PREPARE THE VEGETABLES

1 Trim both ends from each of the medium courgettes and cut the courgettes lengthwise in half.

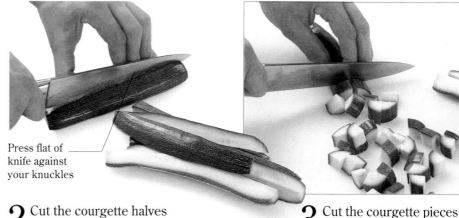

Press flat of knife against your knuckles

2 Cut the courgette halves lengthwise into quarters.

3 Cut the courgette pieces across into 9 mm (⅜ inch) chunks.

4 Bring a medium saucepan of salted water to the boil. Add the courgette chunks and cook until barely tender, 2-3 minutes.

5 Drain the courgette chunks in the colander, rinse with cold water and leave to drain thoroughly.

6 Cut the carrots into chunks like the courgettes. Put the carrots in the medium saucepan, cover with cold water, add salt and bring to the boil.

Carrots should retain their shape and firmness

Protect your fingers with folded cloth or oven gloves

7 Simmer until the carrots are just tender, 8-10 minutes. Drain them in the colander, rinse with cold water and leave to drain thoroughly. Set aside.

8 Bring a small saucepan of salted water to the boil. Add the peas and simmer until tender, 3-8 minutes, depending on their size. Drain them, rinse with cold water and drain again thoroughly. Set aside.

2 MAKE COURGETTE GARNISH

1 Heat the oven to 180°C (350°F, Gas 4). Trim the flower ends of the baby courgettes. Cut each one lengthwise into 4-5 slices, leaving them attached at the stalk end.

2 Butter the baking sheet. Put the courgettes on the sheet, sprinkle with salt and pepper and cover with buttered foil. Bake the courgettes in the heated oven until tender, 15-20 minutes.

3 With your finger and thumb, flatten each sliced courgette to make a fan shape; keep them warm.

3 COOK THE SPAGHETTI AND FINISH THE SAUCE

2 While the spaghetti is cooking, finish the sauce: heat the butter in a large saucepan, add the courgette and carrot chunks and the peas and sauté 1 minute.

Cream provides basis of sauce and enables vegetables to coat pasta

Long feet allow water to drain away completely

3 Add the cream, stir well to mix and heat until simmering.

Saucepan needs to be large enough to hold spaghetti that will be added later

1 Fill the large pan with water, bring to the boil and add 15 ml (1 tbsp) salt. Add the spaghetti and simmer until tender but still chewy, 5-8 minutes, stirring occasionally to prevent sticking. Drain the pasta, rinse with hot water and drain again thoroughly.

Wooden forks help
you to lift and
separate strands

4 Take the pan from the heat, add
the drained spaghetti and toss
to mix with the vegetables
and cream.

5 Add the Parmesan cheese and
toss gently to coat the spaghetti.

🍽 **TO SERVE**
Pile the pasta on 4 warmed individual
plates and garnish each with a
courgette fan.

**Cubes of spring-
time vegetables**
peep out from
spaghetti

Spaghetti glistens
from its light
coating of
cream sauce
and Parmesan

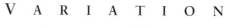

VARIATION

SPAGHETTI VERDE

*Sprigs of broccoli replace the
carrots in Spaghetti with Spring
Vegetables, creating an
attractive medley of green.*

1 Trim the florets from 1 medium
head of broccoli and cut larger florets
into sprigs.
2 Bring a medium pan of salted water
to the boil, add the broccoli and
simmer until tender, 3-5 minutes.
Drain, rinse with cold water and
drain again thoroughly.
3 Sauté the broccoli sprigs
with the peas and courgettes
(omit the carrots) and finish
the sauce as directed.

Baby courgettes,
fanned outwards on
plate, are simple
but effective
garnish

ANNE SAYS
'*If baby courgettes are
not available, you can
substitute 125 g (4 oz)
mangetouts. Trim them
and sauté in about
15 g (½ oz) butter
until barely tender.
Arrange them,
overlapping, in a fan
shape on each serving.*'

QUILLS WITH AUTUMN VEGETABLES

Penne Autunno

 SERVES 6-8 AS AN APPETISER   WORK TIME 40-45 MINUTES*   COOKING TIME 5-8 MINUTES

EQUIPMENT

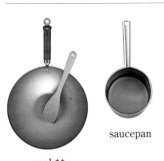

wok**

saucepan

small knife

chef's knife

large pan

slotted spoon

bowls   chopping board

kitchen paper

colander   sieve

** large frying pan can also be used

ANNE SAYS

'*The topping for the pasta is, in essence, a classic stir-fry. This is an ideal way to add new life to leftover vegetables which can be used in place of the squash and aubergine.*'

The rich colours and mellow flavours of autumn star in this simple pasta dish. The sauce is made from yellow squash, ripe red tomatoes and purple aubergine, accented with peppers, onions and garlic.

GETTING AHEAD

The autumn vegetable sauce can be made up to 48 hours ahead and kept refrigerated. Reheat the sauce, cook the pasta and toss them together just before serving.

* plus 30 minutes standing time

metric	SHOPPING LIST	imperial
250 g	yellow squash (see Anne Says above right)	8 oz
2	garlic cloves	2
2	medium onions	2
1	small aubergine	1
	salt and pepper	
250 g	tomatoes	8 oz
1	medium red pepper	1
75 ml	olive oil, more if needed	2 ½ fl oz
500 g	pasta quills	1 lb

INGREDIENTS

yellow squash   onions

aubergine

garlic cloves   tomatoes

red pepper

olive oil

pasta quills

ANNE SAYS

'*Any yellow squash – yellow courgettes or custard marrow as shown here – can be used.*'

ORDER OF WORK

1. **PREPARE THE VEGETABLES**

2. **MAKE THE SAUCE**

3. **COOK THE QUILLS AND FINISH THE DISH**

1 PREPARE THE VEGETABLES

1 Slice the yellow squash, discarding the ends.

2 Finely chop the garlic. Cut the onions in half through root and stem, then thinly slice each half.

Knife must be sharp to cut through peel of aubergine

Salting and draining aubergine in this way helps remove any bitter juices

3 Trim the aubergine and cut it in half lengthwise. Cut the halves lengthwise into wedges. Slice the wedges into 9 mm (³/₈ inch) chunks. Put them in the colander, sprinkle with salt and drain 30 minutes. Rinse the chunks and pat dry with kitchen paper.

4 Peel, seed and chop the tomatoes (see box, page 90). Core and seed the pepper and cut it into strips (see box, below).

HOW TO CORE AND SEED A PEPPER AND CUT IT INTO STRIPS

1 With a chef's knife, cut around the pepper core. Twist the core and then carefully pull it out. Discard the core.

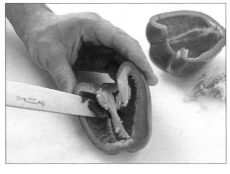

2 Halve the pepper lengthwise. Cut away the protruding ribs and scrape out the seeds. Rinse the pepper under cold running water and pat dry with kitchen paper.

3 Cut each half pepper in half lengthwise, then cut lengthwise again into thin strips.

HOW TO PEEL, SEED AND CHOP TOMATOES

1 With a small knife, cut the core out of each tomato, then turn the tomato over and mark a cross on the base. Immerse the tomatoes in a saucepan of boiling water until the skin curls away from the cross, 8-15 seconds, depending on ripeness.

2 With a slotted spoon, lift the tomatoes out of the water and transfer them to a bowl of cold water.

1 Heat about half of the oil in the wok. Add the aubergine pieces and stir-fry until browned, 3-5 minutes. Transfer them to a bowl with the slotted spoon. Put the squash slices in the wok and stir-fry until browned, about 3 minutes, adding more oil if necessary. Set them aside with the aubergine.

Squeeze over sieve in bowl to catch juices

3 When the tomatoes are cool, drain them and peel off skin.

4 Halve each tomato crosswise like a grapefruit. Squeeze each half firmly in your fist to remove the seeds, scraping off any remaining seeds with the knife.

2 Add the red pepper strips to the wok with a little more oil and sauté, stirring, until they are limp; transfer them to the bowl.

5 Set each tomato half cut side down on the chopping board and slice it. Turn the slices 90° and slice them again.

6 Coarsely chop the tomatoes into rough dice.

3 Heat about 15 ml (1 tbsp) more oil in the wok, add the sliced onions and stir-fry until they are lightly browned, 2-3 minutes.

4 Return the aubergine, squash and red pepper to the wok and add the tomatoes, garlic, salt and pepper. Stir until mixed. Cover and cook until tender, 10-15 minutes. Taste for seasoning. While the sauce is cooking, cook the pasta.

Stir frequently during cooking to prevent vegetables sticking to bottom of wok

V A R I A T I O N

THREE-PEPPER QUILLS

This colourful recipe takes advantage of the wide variety of sweet peppers.

1 Omit the yellow squash and aubergine from Quills with Autumn Vegetables.
2 Core and seed 2 medium red, 2 medium green and 2 medium yellow peppers and cut them into strips (see box, page 89).
3 Sauté the pepper strips in about 45 ml (3 tbsp) vegetable oil, and continue with the sauce as directed.

ANNE SAYS
'The more colours of peppers you use, the more festive the dish.'

3 COOK THE QUILLS AND FINISH THE DISH

1 Fill the large pan with water, bring to the boil and add 15 ml (1 tbsp) salt. Add the quills and simmer until tender but still chewy, 5-8 minutes, or according to packet instructions, stirring occasionally to prevent sticking. Drain the quills in the colander, rinse with hot water and drain again thoroughly.

Red pepper strips are sweet and brightly coloured

Aubergine gives texture and colour contrast

2 Transfer the quills to the wok and toss to mix with the vegetables, heating briefly if needed.

🍴 **TO SERVE**
Pile the pasta on warmed individual plates and serve hot or at room temperature.

CURLY PASTA PESTO SALAD

Fusilli al Pesto

EQUIPMENT

food processor

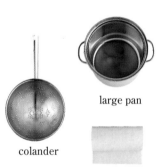
large pan

colander

kitchen paper

large forks

mixing bowl

cheese grater

rubber spatula

Fresh basil combined with garlic, pine nuts, Parmesan cheese and olive oil makes the classic pesto sauce. Here it is tossed with curly pasta to be served warm as an appetiser, but it can also be served as an accompaniment to grilled meats. A food processor is indispensable for the pesto sauce if you want to avoid much hard work pounding by hand.

GETTING AHEAD

The pesto sauce can be made and kept, covered, in the refrigerator up to 48 hours, or it can be frozen. The pasta should be cooked and tossed with the pesto sauce just before serving.

metric	SHOPPING LIST	imperial
60 g	fresh basil	2 oz
6	garlic cloves	6
45 g	pine nuts	1½ oz
125 g	grated Parmesan cheese	4 oz
175 ml	olive oil	6 fl oz
	salt and pepper	
500 g	curly pasta	1 lb
	cherry tomatoes, for decoration (optional)	

INGREDIENTS

fresh basil

garlic cloves

pine nuts

Parmesan cheese

olive oil

curly pasta

ORDER OF WORK

1 MAKE THE PESTO SAUCE

2 COOK THE CURLY PASTA

3 FINISH THE SALAD

1 MAKE THE PESTO SAUCE

1 Strip the leaves from the basil, reserving some small tender sprigs for decoration. Discard the stalks. Rinse the basil leaves and dry on kitchen paper.

Reserve perfect sprigs from tops of basil stalks for decoration

Gently pull leaves away from stalk with fingers

2 Put the basil in the food processor with the garlic, pine nuts, Parmesan cheese and about 45 ml (3 tbsp) of the olive oil. Purée until smooth, scraping down the side of the processor bowl as necessary.

ANNE SAYS
'Pesto sauce is a real treat to have on hand for a variety of uses, such as for tossing with hot spaghetti or stirring into vegetable soup. Double or triple the pesto recipe and freeze the extra in an ice-cube tray for single-serving portions.'

Use rubber spatula to scrape side of processor bowl

Pesto sauce should be thick and emulsified

3 With the blade turning, add the remaining olive oil through the feed tube, pouring it in slowly so the sauce emulsifies.

4 When all the oil has been added, scrape the side of the bowl and process again briefly. Season to taste with salt and pepper.

2 COOK THE CURLY PASTA

1 Fill the large pan with cold water, bring it to the boil and then add 15 ml (1 tbsp) salt.

Add pasta gradually so water doesn't stop boiling

2 Add the curly pasta and simmer until tender but still chewy, 8-10 minutes, or according to packet instructions, stirring occasionally with a large fork to prevent sticking.

Always use very large pan of water to cook pasta

3 Drain the pasta in the colander and rinse under cold running water until the pasta is tepid. Drain again thoroughly.

ALTERNATIVE PASTA SHAPES

Curly pasta is ideal for this dish because the pesto clings well to the spiral shape. You can, however, substitute other dried pasta shapes such as bows, gnocchi or shells.

small shells (conchiglie)

bows (farfalle)

large shells (conchiglie)

gnocchi

3 FINISH THE SALAD

1 Put the pesto sauce in the mixing bowl and add the pasta.

2 Toss the pasta and pesto sauce together with the large forks until the pasta is well coated with the sauce.

🍽 TO SERVE
Pile the salad on individual plates and decorate with the reserved sprigs of basil plus a few cherry tomatoes if desired.

V A R I A T I O N

CURLY PASTA SALAD WITH CORIANDER
The peppery bite of fresh coriander offers a distinctive alternative to the classic basil pesto.

1 Replace the basil with an equal weight of fresh coriander (also known as cilantro and Chinese parsley).
2 Continue as directed for Curly Pasta Pesto Salad.
3 Pile the pasta salad on a serving dish and decorate with sprigs of coriander.

Pesto sauce
clings to shape of curly pasta

Basil sprig
makes pretty decoration

Cherry tomatoes
are bright colour contrast

SPAGHETTI BOLOGNESE

 SERVES 4-6 AS A MAIN COURSE WORK TIME 40-45 MINUTES 🍲 COOKING TIME 1½-2 HOURS

EQUIPMENT

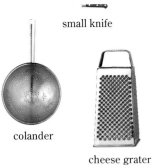

large pan

wooden spoon

chef's knife

sauté pan*

small knife

colander

cheese grater

chopping board

slotted spoon

saucepan

bowl

* frying pan can also be used

Straight from Northern Italy – savoury Bolognese meat sauce served on a mound of hot spaghetti. Made with both minced beef and minced pork, this sauce, or ragù, is delicious with other pasta shapes such as quills, shells and so on.

GETTING AHEAD
The Bolognese sauce can be made and kept, covered, in the refrigerator 24 hours, or it can be frozen. The spaghetti should be cooked just before serving.

metric	SHOPPING LIST	imperial
500 g	spaghetti	1 lb
	grated Parmesan cheese	
	For the Bolognese sauce	
2	medium onions	2
2	garlic cloves	2
1	medium carrot	1
1 kg	tomatoes	2 lb
60 ml	vegetable oil	4 tbsp
375 g	minced beef	12 oz
375 g	minced lean pork	12 oz
250 ml	milk	8 fl oz
375 ml	dry white wine	12 fl oz
15 ml	tomato purée	1 tbsp
1	bouquet garni	1
	salt and pepper	
500 ml	water	16 fl oz

INGREDIENTS

spaghetti

minced beef

minced pork

garlic cloves

onions

tomato purée

dry white wine

tomatoes

carrot

milk

vegetable oil

Parmesan cheese

bouquet garni

ORDER OF WORK

1 MAKE THE BOLOGNESE SAUCE

2 COOK THE SPAGHETTI

How to Dice a Carrot

Diced carrots are an integral part of many flavouring mixtures for sauces and soups.

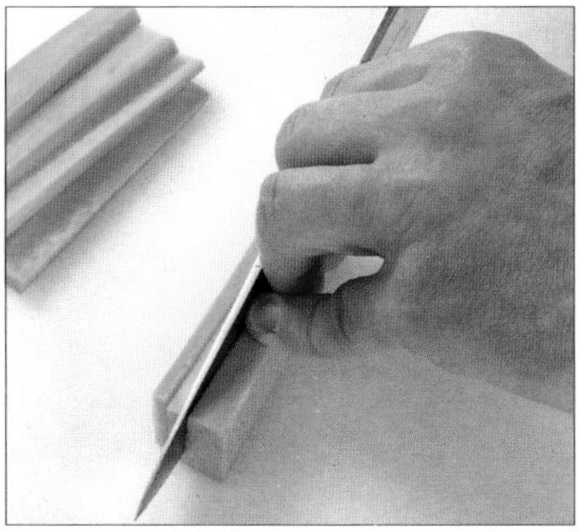

1 Peel the carrot and trim the ends. If the carrot is large, cut it across in half. Trim the sides of the carrot to square them, then cut the carrot lengthwise into thin slices (for large dice, cut into thicker slices).

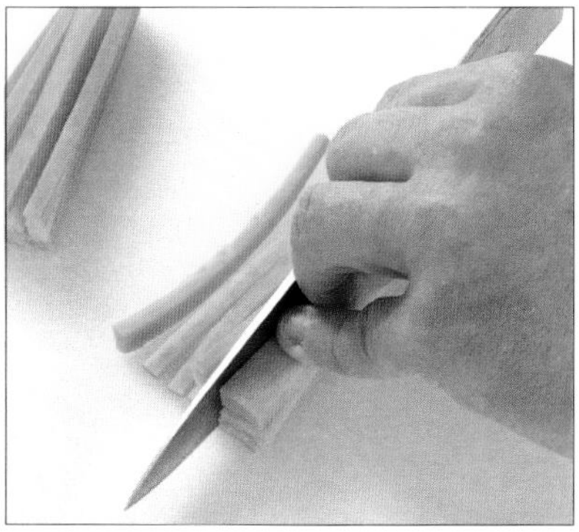

2 Stack the slices and cut them into strips.

3 Cut the strips of carrot across into dice, cutting finely for small dice, thickly for large dice, according to the recipe.

1 Make the Bolognese Sauce

1 Finely chop the onions. Chop the garlic. Chop the carrot into small dice (see box, left).

2 Peel and seed the tomatoes, then chop them fairly coarsely.

3 Heat the oil in the sauté pan, add the chopped onions, garlic and carrot and sauté until soft but not brown, 5-7 minutes, stirring frequently.

Stir vegetables to prevent them sticking to pan

4 Add the minced meats and sauté, stirring, until they lose their pink colour, about 5 minutes.

Break up any lumps in meat with edge of spoon while sautéing

5 Pour in the milk and simmer gently, stirring occasionally, until the liquid has evaporated, about 5 minutes.

ANNE SAYS
'Slow cooking, especially at the start, is the key to a good Bolognese sauce. If the meat boils, it will be tough.'

Flavour of wine will remain after alcohol has evaporated

6 Add the wine and continue simmering until it has evaporated, 8-10 minutes longer.

7 Stir in the tomatoes, tomato purée, bouquet garni, salt and pepper, then add the water and simmer until the sauce is thick, 1½-2 hours, stirring occasionally.

8 Discard the bouquet garni and taste the sauce for seasoning.

2 COOK THE SPAGHETTI

1 Fill the large pan with water, bring to the boil and add 15 ml (1 tbsp) salt. Add the spaghetti and simmer until tender but still chewy, 10-12 minutes, or according to packet instructions, stirring occasionally to prevent sticking. Meanwhile, if necessary, reheat the Bolognese sauce.

ANNE SAYS

'If you are cooking spaghetti or other long pasta, hold it firmly in one hand and immerse one end in the pan of boiling water. As the pasta softens, curl it around until it all falls into the pan. Stir it well to prevent sticking.'

2 Drain the spaghetti in the colander, rinse with hot water and drain again thoroughly.

🍽 **TO SERVE** Pile the hot spaghetti in warmed individual bowls or on plates, spoon over the meat sauce and sprinkle with Parmesan cheese.

V A R I A T I O N

SPAGHETTI WITH SPICY MEAT SAUCE

A racy variation of the traditional Bolognese, here the sauce is laced with chillies.

1 Seed and dice 2 fresh chillies. Add them to the sauce with the tomatoes.
2 For presentation, arrange the spaghetti around the edge of warmed individual plates and spoon the meat sauce in the centre. Garnish the spaghetti with slices of green and red chilli, the meat sauce with a pattern of Parmesan cheese.

Meat sauce with tomatoes and white wine is rich and satisfying

Parmesan cheese, freshly grated, is classic accompaniment for pasta

SHELLS WITH SHELLFISH SAUCE

Conchiglie Pescatore

EQUIPMENT

large pan

large sauté pan

bowls

stiff brush

small knife

chef's knife

large metal spoon

wooden spoon

fine mesh sieve*

chopping board

colander

large saucepan with lid

kitchen paper   rubber gloves

* muslin can also be used

INGREDIENTS

mussels

pasta shells

garlic cloves

onions

mushrooms

raw prawns

scallops

parsley

fresh chillies

olive oil   white wine

Pasta shells and shellfish are natural partners, cooked here with mushrooms, garlic and chillies. In this recipe, a combination of fresh mussels, scallops and prawns is used, but it is not absolutely necessary to include all three if they are not readily available.

ANNE SAYS

'*Any pasta shape can be used here, including fresh or dried plain noodles, and clams or a mixture of mussels and clams can be substituted for the mussels. Clams are prepared in the same way as mussels.*'

GETTING AHEAD

The mussels can be cooked 1-2 hours ahead and the sauce ingredients can also be prepared in advance. However, the pasta and sauce are best cooked just before you are ready to serve them.

metric	SHOPPING LIST	imperial
1 kg	mussels	2 lb
2	small onions	2
175 ml	dry white wine	6 fl oz
125 g	scallops	4 oz
500 g	raw prawns	1 lb
2	garlic cloves	2
125 g	mushrooms	4 oz
2	small fresh chillies	2
1	small bunch of parsley	1
60 ml	olive oil	4 tbsp
	salt and pepper	
500 g	pasta shells	1 lb

ORDER OF WORK

1   **PREPARE THE SHELLFISH SAUCE**

2   **COOK THE SHELLFISH SAUCE AND THE PASTA**

HOW TO CLEAN MUSSELS AND STEAM THEM OPEN

The simplest way to open mussels after washing is to steam them. They can be steamed plain, but often white wine and onion are added for extra flavour, as here. After steaming, discard any mussels that have not opened because they are not safe to eat.

1 Scrub the shells under cold running water with a brush, then scrape off barnacles with a small knife. Discard any mussels that have broken shells or that do not close when tapped.

2 Detach and discard any weed or 'beard' from the mussels. Finely chop the onion.

3 Put the mussels in a large pan, add the white wine and onion, and cover. Cook over high heat, shaking the pan occasionally, just until the shells open, 4-8 minutes. (Cooking time depends on the thickness of shells.)

1 PREPARE THE SHELLFISH SAUCE

1 Clean the mussels and steam them open, together with 1 of the onions and the wine (see box, left). Remove the mussels from their shells, reserving 8-12 in their shells for garnish. Pull off the rubbery ring from around each shelled mussel and discard it.

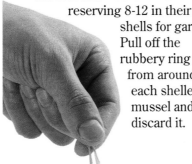

Remove outer ring to make mussel less chewy to eat

Strain cooking liquid to filter out any residual sand and grit

2 Carefully strain the mussel cooking liquid from the pan, leaving any sand behind. Set the liquid aside.

3 Discard the crescent-shaped membrane from the side of each scallop, then cut each one into 2-3 horizontal slices. Peel the prawns.

4 Chop the remaining onion. Chop the garlic. Clean and slice the mushrooms. Seed and finely dice the chillies (see box, page 102). Chop the parsley.

HOW TO SEED AND DICE A FRESH CHILLI

When preparing fresh chillies, wear rubber gloves because the alkaloid, capsaicin, found in the white membrane that holds the seeds, can burn your skin. Wearing gloves will also avoid any danger of capsaicin on your hands getting into your eyes after you have prepared the chillies.

1 Cut the chilli in half lengthwise; discard the core. Scrape out the seeds and cut away the fleshy white 'ribs'.

2 Place each chilli half cut side down and cut lengthwise into very thin strips.

3 Hold the strips together and cut across into very fine dice.

2 COOK THE SHELLFISH SAUCE AND THE PASTA

1 Heat the oil in the sauté pan, add the onion and sauté until soft but not brown, 1-2 minutes. Add the mushrooms, garlic and chilli. Season with salt and pepper and cook, stirring occasionally, until the moisture evaporates, 2-3 minutes.

2 Add the strained cooking liquid from the mussels and boil until the liquid reduces to about 250 ml (8 fl oz), 5-7 minutes.

Cooking liquid from mussels will give sauce more flavour

After boiling, sauce will be be reduced and concentrated

3 Meanwhile, cook the pasta shells: fill the large pan with water, bring to the boil and add 15 ml (1 tbsp) salt. Add the pasta shells and simmer until tender but still chewy, 8-10 minutes, or according to packet instructions, stirring occasionally to prevent sticking. Drain the pasta in the colander, rinse with hot water and drain again thoroughly. Transfer to a warmed large bowl and keep warm.

4 Add the prawns and scallops to the reduced mussel liquid. Stir well and simmer until the prawns begin to turn pink and the scallops become opaque, 2-3 minutes.

5 Stir in the shelled mussels and the mussels in their shells to reheat. Take the sauce from the heat and taste for seasoning. Add the pasta to the shellfish sauce, sprinkle with the chopped parsley and toss gently.

Handle unshelled mussels gently to prevent mussels dislodging

VARIATION

SHELLS WITH PRAWN SAUCE

Prawns, sautéed in olive oil with chillies and spring onions, stand alone in this variation that is ready in minutes.

1 Omit the mussels, scallops, mushrooms, white wine, onions and parsley, and increase the prawns to 750 g (1½ lb).
2 Chop 3 spring onions and sauté them with the garlic and chillies.
3 Add the prawns and cook until pink, 2-3 minutes.
4 Finish the dish as directed.

Mussels in their shells make contrasting, eye-catching garnish

Pasta shells and shellfish have an affinity of size, shape and colour

🍴 **TO SERVE**
Pile the pasta in a large serving bowl and garnish with the mussels in their shells. When transferring the pasta on to individual plates for serving, be sure to divide the shellfish evenly and to garnish each serving with 2 mussels in their shells.

CURLY PASTA WITH WILD MUSHROOMS

Fusilli ai Funghi

 SERVES 4 AS AN APPETISER   WORK TIME 20-25 MINUTES   COOKING TIME 8-10 MINUTES

EQUIPMENT

large pan

small knife

frying pan

chef's knife

wooden spoon

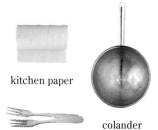

kitchen paper

colander

large forks

chopping board

large bowl

Sautéed wild mushrooms in a cream and white wine sauce top curly pasta. You can use small or large curly pasta, or any other shape, as you prefer. The dish may be served as an appetiser or as an accompaniment to a chicken or veal main course.

GETTING AHEAD

The mushroom sauce can be made and kept, covered, in the refrigerator up to 24 hours. The curly pasta should be cooked and the sauce reheated just before serving.

metric	SHOPPING LIST	imperial
a few	sprigs of parsley	a few
250 g	fresh wild mushrooms (such as shiitake or chanterelles)	8 oz
3	garlic cloves	3
30 g	butter	1 oz
60 ml	dry white wine	4 tbsp
125 ml	double cream	4 fl oz
	salt and pepper	
250 g	curly pasta	8 oz

INGREDIENTS

curly pasta

fresh wild mushrooms

parsley sprigs

butter

garlic cloves

white wine

double cream

ANNE SAYS

'*If you are unable to find fresh wild mushrooms, dried varieties make good substitutes. Some cooks even prefer them because of their intense flavour. Soak 45 g (1½ oz) dried mushrooms in a bowl of warm water until soft and plump, about 30 minutes. Drain them and continue as directed for fresh wild mushrooms.*'

ORDER OF WORK

1   MAKE THE MUSHROOM SAUCE

2   COOK THE CURLY PASTA AND FINISH THE DISH

1 MAKE THE MUSHROOM SAUCE

1 Chop the parsley. Clean and slice the mushrooms (see box, right). Peel and chop the garlic (see box, page 106).

2 Melt the butter in the frying pan, then add the garlic and mushrooms. Cook until most of the liquid has evaporated, about 5 minutes, stirring frequently.

3 Add the white wine, stir to mix and reduce until no liquid remains, stirring frequently.

4 Stir in the cream and heat until boiling, then simmer 2 minutes. Season to taste with salt and pepper. Remove from the heat and keep warm.

Cream is traditionally used with curly pasta because it clings to twisted shape

Mushroom mixture should be quite dry before cream is added

HOW TO CLEAN AND SLICE MUSHROOMS

Mushrooms need to be cleaned carefully if they are dirty. Be sure to rinse them in water 1-2 seconds only; do not soak them because they quickly become waterlogged.

1 Remove any earth from the mushrooms; if using wild mushrooms, pick them over well to remove any twigs. With a small knife, trim the stalks. For cultivated mushrooms, trim the stalks just level with the caps.

2 Wipe the mushrooms clean with damp kitchen paper or a cloth. If they are very dirty, plunge them into cold water, swirl them around and lift them out to drain in a colander.

3 To slice, hold the mushroom stem side down and cut vertically with a chef's knife into slices of the required thickness. Smaller mushrooms, such as chanterelles, are often left whole.

HOW TO PEEL AND CHOP GARLIC

The strength of garlic varies with its age and dryness; use more when it is very fresh.

1 To separate the garlic cloves, crush the whole bulb with the heels of your hands. Alternatively, pull a garlic clove from the bulb with your fingers.

2 To peel the clove, lightly crush it with the flat of a chef's knife to loosen the skin. Peel off the skin with your fingers.

3 To crush the clove, set the flat side of the knife on top and strike firmly with your fist. Finely chop the garlic with the knife, moving the blade back and forth.

2 COOK THE CURLY PASTA AND FINISH THE DISH

Add pasta to pan when water is at rolling boil

1 Fill the large pan with water, bring to the boil and add 7.5 ml (1½ tsp) salt. Add the curly pasta and simmer until tender but still chewy, about 8-10 minutes, or according to packet instructions, stirring occasionally to prevent sticking.

2 Drain the pasta in the colander, rinse with hot water and drain again thoroughly. Transfer the hot pasta to the warmed large bowl.

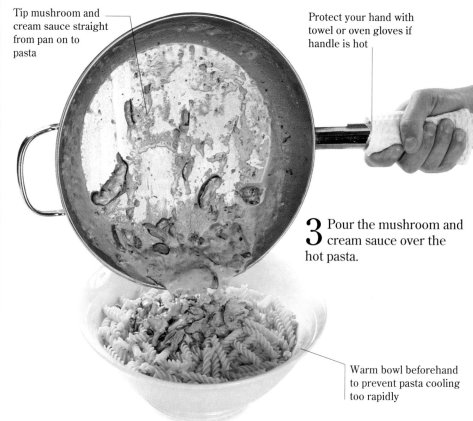

Tip mushroom and cream sauce straight from pan on to pasta

Protect your hand with towel or oven gloves if handle is hot

3 Pour the mushroom and cream sauce over the hot pasta.

Warm bowl beforehand to prevent pasta cooling too rapidly

Gently lift pasta so that sauce runs underneath

4 Sprinkle with most of the chopped parsley and toss to combine, using the large forks.

🍽 **TO SERVE**
Pile the pasta on warmed individual plates, distributing the mushrooms evenly, and sprinkle with the remaining parsley.

Large wooden forks are gentle for tossing cooked pasta and enable you to dig down into bowl

Wild mushrooms have delicious flavour

V A R I A T I O N
CURLY PASTA WITH HERBY MUSHROOMS

Fresh herbs take the place of cream, giving this dish quite a different character and a lower calorie count. Boletus, chanterelles and oyster mushrooms are especially good cooked this way.

1 Chop a few sprigs each of fresh sage, thyme and rosemary. Add the chopped herbs to the sauce at the same time as the wine.
   2 Omit the cream from the mushroom sauce.
      3 Toss the pasta and sauce together and serve on warmed individual plates, as directed in the main recipe.

Spirals are teased out to give finished dish 'composed' look

ANGEL HAIR WITH PRAWNS, ASPARAGUS AND SESAME

 SERVES 4 OR 6   WORK TIME 25-30 MINUTES   COOKING TIME 2-3 MINUTES

EQUIPMENT

small knife   chef's knife

chopping board

wooden spoon

large forks

wok with stirrer*

colander

small frying pan

large pan

large saucepan

large frying pan can also be used

Rapid cooking is the essence of this Oriental-style dish. The pasta is tossed with stir-fried prawns and asparagus, flavoured with ginger and garlic, then topped with toasted sesame seeds. Use the youngest, thinnest green asparagus, so the flavour is intense and the spears are very tender.

GETTING AHEAD

The sauce ingredients can be prepared 1-2 hours ahead, but the sauce and pasta are best if cooked just before serving.

metric	SHOPPING LIST	imperial
250 g	asparagus	8 oz
	salt and pepper	
30 ml	sesame seeds	2 tbsp
3	garlic cloves	3
2	spring onions	2
500 g	raw prawns	1 lb
1	walnut-sized piece of fresh root ginger	1
250 g	angel hair pasta	8 oz
60 ml	vegetable oil	4 tbsp
45 ml	dry sherry	3 tbsp
15 ml	sesame oil	1 tbsp

INGREDIENTS

angel hair pasta

raw prawns

asparagus

vegetable oil

sesame oil

sesame seeds

fresh root ginger

garlic cloves

dry sherry

spring onions

ORDER OF WORK

1. **PREPARE THE SAUCE INGREDIENTS**

2. **COOK THE ANGEL HAIR PASTA**

3. **MAKE THE SAUCE AND FINISH THE DISH**

1 PREPARE THE SAUCE INGREDIENTS

1 With the small knife, trim off the tough shoots along the asparagus stalks. Cut off the ends of the stalks, which may be woody.

ANNE SAYS
'If the asparagus is larger and more mature, you will need to peel the spears with a vegetable peeler, starting just below the tips of the spears and working towards the ends.'

2 Fill the saucepan with water, bring to the boil and add salt. Add the asparagus and simmer until barely tender, 3-5 minutes. Drain the asparagus in the colander and rinse under cold running water. Drain again thoroughly.

3 Trim off about 5 cm (2 inches) of the asparagus tips and reserve them. Cut the asparagus stalks into 2 cm (³/₄ inch) pieces.

4 To toast the sesame seeds, heat the small frying pan over moderate heat, add the seeds and toast them, stirring occasionally, until lightly browned, 2-3 minutes.

5 Chop the garlic. Trim the white ends off the spring onions and reserve for another dish; cut the green part into 5 mm (¹/₄ inch) thick slices on the diagonal. Peel and devein the prawns (see box, page 110). Peel and chop the root ginger (see box, below).

HOW TO PEEL AND CHOP FRESH ROOT GINGER

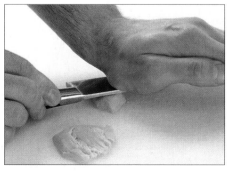

1 With a small knife, peel the skin from the root ginger. Using a chef's knife, slice the root ginger, cutting across the fibrous grain.

2 Place the knife flat on each slice of root ginger and crush with the heel of your hand.

3 Finely chop the slices of ginger with the chef's knife.

HOW TO PEEL AND DEVEIN PRAWNS

Prawns have an intestinal vein along the back that should be removed before cooking.

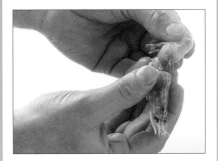

1 If the head is on the prawn, pinch it off.

2 Peel the shell off the prawn with your fingers.

3 With a small knife, make a shallow cut along the back of the prawn.

4 Gently pull out the dark intestinal vein and discard it.

2 COOK THE ANGEL HAIR PASTA

1 Fill the large pan with water, bring to the boil and add 7.5 ml (1½ tsp) salt. Add the pasta and simmer until tender but still chewy, 2-3 minutes, stirring occasionally to prevent sticking.

2 Drain the pasta in the colander, rinse with hot water and drain again thoroughly.

3 MAKE THE SAUCE AND FINISH THE DISH

1 Heat the oil in the wok, add the garlic, root ginger and prawns, and stir-fry until the prawns just begin to turn pink, 1-2 minutes.

2 Add the sherry and cook, stirring constantly, until slightly reduced and the prawns are a deeper pink, 1-2 minutes.

3 Add the asparagus stalks to the wok and stir to combine with the prawn mixture.

Round bottom and sloping sides make wok ideal shape for cooking cut-up pieces of food quickly

4 Add the angel hair pasta and toss to mix using the large forks.

5 Add the spring onions and toss until hot, 30-60 seconds. Remove from the heat, sprinkle with the sesame oil, then taste for seasoning. Pile the hot pasta mixture on warmed individual plates and sprinkle the toasted sesame seeds on top.

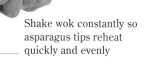

Shake wok constantly so asparagus tips reheat quickly and evenly

6 Wipe the wok clean. Reheat the asparagus tips in the wok 30 seconds.

VARIATION

ANGEL HAIR WITH SMOKED OYSTERS, ASPARAGUS AND SESAME

Smoked oysters are a good off-the-shelf alternative when fresh prawns are unavailable.

1 Omit the prawns and use three 125 g (4 oz) cans of smoked oysters.
2 Drain the oysters and pat dry with kitchen paper.
3 Sauté the oysters with the garlic and root ginger 1 minute, then continue with the recipe as directed.

Juicy prawns
are flavoured with ginger and garlic

Asparagus tips
arranged in threes make effective decoration around edge of plate

 **TO SERVE**
Arrange the asparagus tips around the pasta and take to the table immediately.

FRESH TUNA PASTA SALAD NICOISE

 SERVES 6 AS A MAIN COURSE   WORK TIME 35-40 MINUTES*   COOKING TIME 8-10 MINUTES

EQUIPMENT

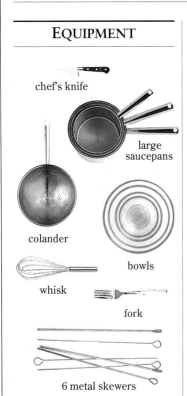

chef's knife

large saucepans

colander

bowls

whisk

fork

6 metal skewers

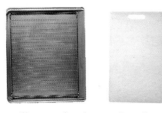

grill pan and rack

chopping board

metal spoon

large forks

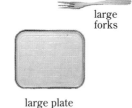

large plate

The familiar ingredients of a Salade Niçoise – tuna, green beans, tomatoes and black olives – are combined on a background of pasta bows. Other pasta shapes can also be used.

— GETTING AHEAD —

The dressing can be kept, covered, at room temperature up to 24 hours, and the tuna kebabs can be marinated up to 6 hours. The beans and pasta should be cooked and the tuna grilled just before serving.

*plus 1 hour marinating time

INGREDIENTS

fresh tuna steaks   pasta bows

cherry tomatoes

French beans

anchovy fillets

lemon juice

fresh thyme

garlic cloves

Dijon mustard

olive oil   balsamic vinegar

black olives

metric	SHOPPING LIST	imperial
1 kg	fresh tuna steaks, cut 2.5 cm (1 inch) thick	2 lb
750 g	French beans	1½ lb
500 g	pasta bows	1 lb
	vegetable oil for grill rack	
500 g	cherry tomatoes	1 lb
100 g	stoned black olives	3½ oz
	For the marinade and dressing	
8	anchovy fillets	8
1	sprig of fresh thyme	1
2	garlic cloves	2
60 ml	lemon juice	4 tbsp
15 ml	balsamic or red wine vinegar	1 tbsp
5 ml	Dijon mustard	1 tsp
	black pepper	
250 ml	olive oil	8 fl oz

ORDER OF WORK

1 PREPARE AND MARINATE THE TUNA

2 PREPARE THE FRENCH BEANS

3 COOK THE PASTA BOWS

4 GRILL THE TUNA KEBABS

1 PREPARE AND MARINATE THE TUNA

1 First make the marinade: chop the anchovy fillets. Chop the thyme. Chop the garlic. Put all of these ingredients in a small bowl and stir to combine.

2 Add the lemon juice, vinegar, mustard, anchovy, thyme, garlic and pepper and whisk together until evenly mixed.

3 Slowly pour the olive oil into the anchovy mixture in a thin, steady stream, whisking constantly, so that the mixture emulsifies and thickens.

ANNE SAYS
'*Any firm fish such as swordfish or halibut can be substituted for the tuna. You can also substitute canned tuna, but use only good-quality tuna, packed in water. Do not grill it, but simply drain and pile it on the plate with the other ingredients.*'

Spear skewer through centre of each cube of tuna

4 Discard any skin from the tuna steaks, then cut the tuna into 2.5 cm (1 inch) cubes.

Space tuna cubes evenly on skewers without squashing them

5 Thread the tuna cubes on to the skewers and set on the plate. Spoon about 75 ml (5 tbsp) of the marinade over the tuna, cover and leave to marinate in the refrigerator 1 hour, turning the skewers occasionally. While the tuna is marinating, prepare the beans and cook the pasta.

2 PREPARE THE FRENCH BEANS

1 With your fingers, snap the ends off the beans; rinse the beans in the colander. Bring a large pan of salted water to the boil. Add the beans and cook until tender but still firm, about 5-8 minutes for medium beans; tiny beans may take as little as 3-4 minutes, large beans up to 12 minutes.

ANNE SAYS
'Rinsing just-cooked green vegetables with cold water stops them cooking and helps maintain their bright green colour.'

2 Drain the beans in the colander, rinse under cold running water and drain again thoroughly.

Colander with feet can be set in sink to make draining and rinsing very easy

3 Put the beans in a bowl, add 75 ml (5 tbsp) of the dressing and toss together with the large forks. Set aside.

3 COOK THE PASTA BOWS

2 Put the pasta in a bowl, add about 75 ml (5 tbsp) of the dressing and toss well. Set aside.

Dressing should be whisked until thick before spooning over pasta

1 Bring a large pan of water to the boil and add 15 ml (1 tbsp) salt. Add the pasta and simmer until tender but still chewy, 8-10 minutes or according to packet instructions, stirring occasionally to prevent sticking. Drain and rinse under cold running water until tepid. Drain again.

Pasta is warm when dressing is added so flavours will be absorbed

4 GRILL THE TUNA KEBABS

1 Heat the grill; oil the grill rack. Transfer the tuna kebabs to the rack and grill them about 7.5 cm (3 inches) from the heat 2 minutes. Turn the kebabs, baste with about 45 ml (3 tbsp) of the dressing and grill 2 minutes longer. The tuna should be brown on the outside but slightly translucent in the centre. While the tuna is being grilled, arrange the pasta on 6 individual plates, with the tomatoes and French beans.

🍴 TO SERVE

Slide the tuna into the centre of the salad, using the fork to loosen. Spoon the remaining dressing over all, especially the tomatoes. Add the olives. The tuna should be hot; the salad at room temperature.

Cherry tomatoes provide sweet-tart accent and bright colour

Tuna cubes are tender and full of flavour

French beans are lightly cooked to keep their crunch

V A R I A T I O N

VEGETABLE PASTA SALAD NICOISE

Cubes of aubergine replace the tuna in Fresh Tuna Pasta Salad Niçoise for an unusual version of the Mediterranean classic.

1 Trim the stalk end off 1 large aubergine (about 300 g/10 oz) and cut it in half lengthwise. Cut the halves lengthwise into 2.5 cm (1 inch) wedge-shaped slices; cut the slices into 2.5 cm (1 inch) cubes.
2 If you like, peel and thickly slice 4-5 plump garlic cloves.
3 Thread the aubergine cubes and garlic slices (if using) on to skewers, pushing the skewers through the aubergine skin to keep it from falling apart as it cooks; marinate as for tuna.
4 Grill the marinated aubergine until tender, 5-8 minutes, turning once.
5 Prepare the other salad ingredients and the pasta as directed, cutting the beans and tomatoes in half.
6 Slide the aubergine from the skewers on to the plates, garnish with salad leaves and serve at room temperature.

ANNE SAYS
'*For an outdoor treat while the weather is warm, marinate the tuna as directed and cook it on the barbecue. To simplify presentation, you can toss together the pasta, beans, tomatoes and olives with three-quarters of the dressing.*'

SICILIAN MACARONI WITH SARDINES, FENNEL AND RAISINS

Macaroni alle Sarde

 SERVES 4-6 AS A MAIN COURSE　 WORK TIME 40-45 MINUTES　COOKING TIME 10-12 MINUTES

EQUIPMENT

large pan

frying pan

medium saucepan

chef's knife

large forks

wooden spoon

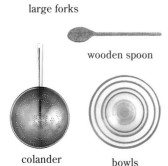

colander

bowls

chopping board

baking sheet

INGREDIENTS

canned sardines in oil

macaroni

bulb fennel

onions

pine nuts

raisins

olive oil

This unusual main course combines sardines, fennel, raisins, crunchy pine nuts and olive oil, all tossed together to create a most distinctive flavour. In Sicily, cooks use fresh sardines and the wild fennel native to their countryside. On a hot summer's day, Sicilian macaroni is excellent served at room temperature.

GETTING AHEAD

The sardine topping can be prepared up to 24 hours ahead and kept, covered, in the refrigerator. The macaroni should be cooked and the dish finished just before serving.

metric	SHOPPING LIST	imperial
500 g	bulb fennel	1 lb
	salt and pepper	
45 g	pine nuts	1½ oz
2	medium onions	2
125 ml	olive oil	4 fl oz
375 g	canned sardines in oil	12 oz
45 g	raisins	1½ oz
375 g	macaroni	12 oz

ORDER OF WORK

1 PREPARE THE SARDINE TOPPING

2 COOK THE SARDINE TOPPING

3 COOK THE MACARONI AND FINISH THE DISH

1 PREPARE THE SARDINE TOPPING

1 Wash the fennel bulbs and trim off the woody bases and dry tops.

2 Cut fennel bulbs in half lengthwise, then slice crosswise.

Drain fennel cooking liquid into pasta pan to use for cooking pasta later

HOW TO TOAST PINE NUTS

Heat the oven to 190°C (375°F, Gas 5). Spread the pine nuts on a baking sheet and bake in the heated oven until evenly brown, 5-8 minutes.

ANNE SAYS
'Toasting intensifies the flavour of pine nuts.'

3 Fill the saucepan with salted water and bring to the boil. Add the fennel and simmer until just tender, about 5 minutes. Drain the fennel in the colander held over the large pan, and reserve the cooking liquid.

4 Allow the fennel to cool, then chop it coarsely. Toast the pine nuts (see box, left).

2 COOK THE SARDINE TOPPING

1 Thinly slice the onions (see box, below). Heat the oil in the frying pan, add the onions and sauté until soft, 3-5 minutes.

2 Drain the sardines. Reserve 4 for garnish and add the rest to the pan. Cook, crushing the fish against the bottom of the pan, 2-3 minutes.

HOW TO SLICE AN ONION

1 Peel the onion and trim the top, leaving the root intact. Cut the onion in half lengthwise.

2 Put one half, cut side down, on a chopping board. Holding the onion firmly, slice it crosswise, starting at the top and guiding the knife with bent fingers. Discard the root when you reach it. Repeat with other onion half.

ANNE SAYS
'The root helps hold the onion together during slicing.'

3 Add the fennel, raisins and toasted pine nuts and stir to mix. Heat thoroughly, 3-5 minutes. Season to taste and keep warm.

Toasted pine nuts will keep their crunch in sardine topping

3 COOK THE MACARONI AND FINISH THE DISH

1 Bring the fennel cooking liquid in the large pan to the boil. (If necessary, add water to the cooking liquid so that you will have enough to cook the pasta.) Add the macaroni and simmer until tender but still chewy, 10-12 minutes, or according to packet instructions, stirring occasionally to prevent sticking.

2 Drain the pasta in the colander, rinse with hot water and drain again thoroughly. Transfer the pasta to a warmed large bowl, add about half of the sardine topping and toss thoroughly to mix.

Sardine topping is tossed into macaroni to coat thoroughly

🍴 TO SERVE

Pile the macaroni on warmed individual plates, top with the remaining sardine mixture and garnish with the reserved whole sardines.

Sardine garnish tops piquant macaroni dish

VARIATION

BAKED MACARONI WITH CHEESE, FENNEL AND RAISINS

In this variation of Sicilian Macaroni, the sardines are replaced by ricotta cheese. Instead of tossing the pasta with the topping, it is layered with the cheese mixture and baked in the oven, topped with mozzarella. If you like, you can omit the raisins.

1 Prepare the topping as directed, omitting the sardines. Take from the heat and, when cooled, stir in 500 g (1 lb) ricotta cheese. Season well.
2 Cook and drain the macaroni as directed.
3 Heat the oven to 180°C (350°F, Gas 4). Butter a baking dish.
4 Spread about half of the macaroni in the baking dish and cover with about half of the ricotta topping. Repeat the layers of macaroni and topping.

5 Slice 250 g (8 oz) mozzarella cheese and lay the slices evenly over the top.
6 Bake in the heated oven until the mozzarella has melted and is golden brown and the macaroni is very hot, 15-20 minutes.

CORSICAN MACARONI WITH BEEF STEW

Stufatu

 SERVES 4-6 AS A MAIN COURSE   WORK TIME 25-30 MINUTES   COOKING TIME 2 ¾ HOURS

EQUIPMENT

chef's knife

ovenproof sauté pan

colander

cheese grater

large heatproof bowl

slotted spoon

kitchen paper

shallow dish

large pan

large metal spoon

bowl

chopping board

In this Corsican dish, a savoury beef stew is tossed with macaroni and topped with a sprinkling of Parmesan cheese.

GETTING AHEAD

The beef stew can be prepared up to 48 hours ahead and kept, covered, in the refrigerator. The macaroni should be cooked and the stew reheated just before serving.

metric	SHOPPING LIST	imperial
2	onions	2
125 g	mushrooms	4 oz
4	garlic cloves	4
1	sprig of fresh rosemary or 5 ml (1 tsp) dried	1
1 kg	stewing beef	2 lb
30 g	flour	1 oz
	salt and pepper	
30 ml	vegetable oil	2 tbsp
1	bouquet garni	1
10 ml	ground cinnamon	2 tsp
300 ml	dry white wine	½ pint
500 g	macaroni	1 lb
30 g	grated Parmesan cheese, to serve	1 oz

INGREDIENTS

macaroni

stewing beef

vegetable oil

mushrooms

Parmesan cheese

white wine

onions

garlic cloves

bouquet garni

fresh rosemary

flour

ground cinnamon

ORDER OF WORK

1 PREPARE THE INGREDIENTS

2 COOK THE BEEF STEW

3 COOK THE MACARONI AND FINISH THE DISH

1 PREPARE THE INGREDIENTS

1 Cut the onions in half, then slice them. Clean and slice the mushrooms. Chop the garlic.

2 Strip the leaves from the sprig of rosemary and pile them on the chopping board.

3 Cut the rosemary leaves into small pieces, then chop finely.

4 Cut the stewing beef into 2 cm (³/₄ inch) cubes.

Beef should be lean and trimmed of any fat before being cubed

2 COOK THE BEEF STEW

1 Stir together the flour with 5 ml (1 tsp) salt and a good pinch of pepper in the shallow dish. Add the beef cubes a few at a time and toss so they are thoroughly coated. Pat off the excess flour to obtain an even coating.

2 Heat the oil in the sauté pan, add the beef cubes in batches and brown them well on all sides. Remove the beef cubes with the slotted spoon.

! TAKE CARE !
Do not crowd the beef in the pan, otherwise it will give up its juices and start to steam rather than fry.

3 Add the sliced onions to the hot oil in the pan and cook until they are lightly browned, 3-5 minutes, stirring frequently with the slotted spoon.

4 Return the beef to the pan with the garlic and stir to mix with the onions.

5 Stir in the mushrooms, bouquet garni, rosemary, cinnamon, salt and pepper. Add the white wine.

Handles must be ovenproof because beef will be cooked in sauté pan in oven

6 Cover and cook over very low heat, stirring occasionally, 30 minutes.

ANNE SAYS
'*For a more traditional, but less Corsican, beef stew, add chopped carrots and peeled baby onions about halfway through cooking.*'

7 Heat the oven to 180°C (350°F, Gas 4). Add enough water to cover the meat. Cover the pan again and cook in the oven, stirring occasionally, until the meat is very tender and falling apart, about 2 hours. Add more water during cooking if the meat seems dry.

Use slotted spoon to lift out bouquet garni

8 Discard the bouquet garni and taste the stew for seasoning. If you like an extra thick gravy, remove the meat and reduce the cooking liquid to the desired thickness.

3 COOK THE MACARONI AND FINISH THE DISH

1 Fill the large pan with water, bring to the boil and add 15 ml (1 tbsp) salt. Add the macaroni and simmer until tender but still chewy, 10-12 minutes, or according to packet instructions, stirring occasionally to prevent sticking. Drain the pasta, rinse with hot water and drain again.

Bowl used for mixing should be warmed beforehand so pasta does not cool

2 Put the pasta in the warmed heat-proof bowl, spoon over about half of the beef stew and toss to mix. Pile the macaroni in warmed individual shallow bowls, add the remaining stew and serve immediately, with the Parmesan served separately.

Macaroni is tossed with half of beef stew so it is juicy

Beef cubes, cooked until tender with vegetables, wine, herbs and cinnamon, make a delicious partner for macaroni

V A R I A T I O N

MACARONI WITH LAMB STEW

The favourite Mediterranean meat is lamb, here made into a stew for a version of Corsican Macaroni. This modern presentation shows the pasta and meat stew side by side, rather than tossed together as in the main recipe.

1 Replace the stewing beef with an equal quantity of lean boneless lamb shoulder meat.
2 Substitute 175 g (6 oz) whole stoned green olives for the mushrooms, adding them about 10 minutes before the end of cooking.
3 Omit the Parmesan cheese.

PASTA KNOW-HOW

All pasta is based on starch dough (the Italian word 'pasta' means paste). There are two interchangeable types, one is made with egg, the other is simply mixed with water. Not surprisingly, pasta made with egg is considered the best, particularly when it is freshly made. The dough can be left plain, or flavoured and coloured with ingredients such as tomato purée or chopped spinach.

CHOOSING PASTA

The best commercial fresh or dried pasta is made with high gluten flour and is labelled '100% pure durum wheat' or 'pure semolina'. It should have a lively wheat flavour. Egg pasta should be light gold in colour, with a slightly rough texture. Dusty crumbs in the bottom of the packet indicate pasta may be stale.

SHAPES

Pasta can be long, short, thin, wide, flat, curly, ribbed or tubular to mention just a few of the possibilities. When substituting one pasta for another, it is best to stick with similar shapes. For example, when tagliatelle is specified you can replace it with spaghetti but not rigatoni. This is because specific sauces complement certain shapes. Both thin and thick string pastas such as spaghetti, linguine and vermicelli go well with strongly-flavoured tomato sauces. Spaghetti, which is the thickest, can also support butter and cream sauces, but the thinner vermicelli and linguine are best with lighter seafood sauces or those based on olive oil. Angel hair pasta, thinnest of all, is best tossed simply in oil with a piquant ingredient or two.

Short, stubby pastas go well with meat sauce, while shells and twists that collect plenty of sauce without sticking together are excellent in salads. Stuffed pastas should be paired with a subtle sauce because the main seasoning is in the filling.

FLOUR FOR PASTA

Flour that is good for pasta contains plenty of gluten, the protein that glues dough together and makes it firm and resilient. Strong plain flour has a high gluten content, and I find it works well for pasta dough, although ordinary plain (unbleached) flour can also be used. Semolina flour,

intended specifically for pasta, is also available and has a particularly high gluten content. It makes an elastic dough that can be hard to roll out by hand, but the pasta remains agreeably chewy after boiling.

SERVINGS

A half kilo or one pound of fresh or dried pasta will serve six to eight as an appetiser, or four as a main course when garnished with a simple sauce. If a filling or garnish is rich or elaborate, use less pasta. In some of the recipes in this book you will find a range of servings is given (for example, 4 or 6); the lower figure is for main-course servings, the higher figure is for appetiser servings.

STORING

Home-made pasta should be sprinkled lightly with flour or fine cornmeal, left to dry one to two hours, then packed in plastic bags. It can be refrigerated up to 48 hours, or frozen up to two months. Be sure the pasta is thoroughly dried before wrapping or it will stick during storage.

The length of time layered and filled fresh pasta can be kept in the refrigerator depends on the type of filling, but stuffed pastas freeze well.

Commercial dried pasta may be stored six months or more at room temperature.

COOKING

Pasta is almost always boiled in salted water, although stock is used occasionally. A large quantity of liquid should be used so the pasta pieces swim without touching and sticking together; large pasta such as lasagne and cannelloni may need cooking in two batches.

To boil pasta, allow 5 litres (8 pints) of water for the first 500 g (1 lb) of pasta, increasing the quantity of water by 1 litre (1 ²/₃ pints) for each additional 250 g (8 oz) pasta. A tablespoon of salt is needed for 500 g (1 lb) of pasta; add it after the water has been brought to the boil. A tablespoon of oil added to the water will help keep the pasta from sticking, and the water from boiling over.

For small or finely-cut pasta such as fettuccine, use a deep pan such as a stockpot. If you like, immerse a pasta drainer inside the pan before adding the pasta, so it is easy to lift out and drain after cooking, leaving the water to be used again. For larger pasta such as lasagne, a shallow pan such as a sauté pan or roasting tin is better so the pieces do not stick together. To avoid damaging pasta pieces, carefully remove them with a draining spoon.

When the water boils, add the pasta, stirring from time to time as it cooks so it does not stick together. Dried long pasta, such as spaghetti, must be bent slowly into the water as it softens until it is completely covered.

Freshly-made pasta cooks very quickly so test as soon as it comes back to the boil. Thin dried pasta should be tested after three minutes boiling, while larger shapes can take up to 12 minutes to cook.

TESTING AND DRAINING

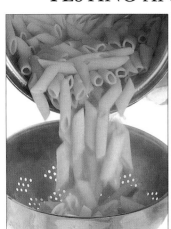

Pasta should be cooked until it is tender but still chewy. Taste a piece: it should be *'al dente'* or firm to the bite with no hard centre or raw taste. When you nip it with a thumb nail, it should be slightly resistant. If it is to be baked further after boiling, take care not to overcook pasta. As soon as it is cooked, drain and rinse the pasta to wash away the starch. Use hot water if the pasta is to be served hot, or cold water if it is to be used as a salad or cooked again as in baked pasta.

! TAKE CARE !
Be sure to use cooked pasta at once as directed because it will stick together if left to stand.

HOW-TO BOXES

*There are pictures of all preparation steps for each **Perfect Pasta** recipe. Some basic techniques are general to a number of recipes; they are shown in extra detail in these special 'how-to' boxes:*

INDEX

ACKNOWLEDGEMENTS

Photographer David Murray
Photographer's Assistant Jules Selmes

Chef Eric Treuille
Cookery Consultant Linda Collister
Home Economist Annie Nichols

UK Editor José Northey
Indexer Sally Poole

Typesetting Rowena Feeny
Text film by Disc To Print (UK) Limited

Production Consultant Lorraine Baird

Carroll & Brown Limited
would like to thank ICTC (081-568-4179)
for supplying the Cuisinox Elysee pans used throughout
the book and The Kitchenware Merchants Limited
for providing the Le Creuset cookware.
Moulinex/Swan Holdings Limited supplied
the electric mincer.

Anne Willan
would like to thank her chief editor
Cynthia Nims and associate editor Kate Krader
for their vital help with writing the book and
researching and testing the recipes,
aided by Kelly McNabb and La Varenne's
chefs and trainees.